WHAT'S COOKING
low fat

Kathryn Hawkins

THUNDER BAY
P·R·E·S·S

First published in the United States in 1998 by
Thunder Bay Press
An imprint of the Advantage Publishers Group
5880 Oberlin Drive, San Diego, CA 92121-4794
www.advantagebooksonline.com

Library of Congress Cataloging in Publication Data

Hawkins, Kathryn.
What's Cooking? Low Fat. Kathryn Hawkins.
  p. cm.
Includes index
ISBN: 1-57145-146-3
  1.Cookery, Low Fat diet --Recipes   1. Title
RM237.7.11397   1998
641.5638--dc21   98-16097
                                                                        CIP

Printed in Indonesia
4 5 6 01 02 03

Produced by Haldane Mason, London

Acknowledgments
Art Director: Ron Samuels
Editorial Director: Sydney Francis
Editorial Consultant: Christopher Fagg
Managing Editor: Jo-Anne Cox
Editor: Lydia Darbyshire
Design: Digital Artworks Partnership Ltd
Photography: Iain Bagwell
Home Economist: Kathryn Hawkins
Nutritional information: Anne Sheasby and Annette Yates

Note
Unless otherwise stated, milk is assumed to be full fat, eggs are medium,
and pepper is freshly ground black pepper. The calorie counts and fat content analysis
do not include the serving suggestions.

Contents

Introduction

No one who has more than a passing interest in their health can be unaware of the problems associated with a diet that contains too much fat. A high level of fat consumption is implicated in obesity—and all that that entails—coronary disease, diabetes, and even cancer. The message that we should all cut down on the fat in our diets is reinforced every time we go shopping, and it is almost impossible to walk around a supermarket without being beset on all sides by labels proclaiming low-fat this, reduced-fat that, and no-fat the other.

Cutting the amount of fat in our diets is, of course, an effective way to lose weight, simply because it will reduce the number of calories we consume, as well as reducing the likelihood that we will contract a serious disease. However, before we cut fat out of our lives completely, it is important to remember that we all need to include a certain amount of fat in our daily intake of food if our bodies are to function properly. Essential fatty acids are needed to build cell membranes and for other vital bodily functions. Our brain tissue, nerve sheaths, and bone marrow need fat, for example, and we all need fat to protect vital organs, such as our liver, kidneys, and heart.

Nutritionists suggest that we should aim to cut our intake of fat to 27-30 percent of our total daily calorie intake. If your average diet totals 2,000 calories, this will mean eating no more than approximately 2¾ ounces of fat a day. As a guide, bear in mind that most people consume about 40 percent of their daily calories in the form of fat. Remember, however, that if you are being treated for any medical condition, you must discuss with your doctor or other professional the changes you propose making in your diet before you begin your new regime.

When you are thinking about reducing your intake of fat, it is important to know that fats can be broadly divided into saturated and unsaturated fat. Saturated fats are those that are solid at room temperature, and they are found mainly in animal products—butter and cheese, high-fat meats (sausages, pâté, fatty bacon), cakes, chocolate, potato chips, cookies, coconut, and hydrogenated (hardened) vegetable or fish oils. Unsaturated fats are healthier—but they are still fats. Your target should be a reduction to 8 percent of your daily calories in the form of saturated facts, with the remainder in the form of unsaturated fats. These are usually liquid at room temperature and come from vegetable sources—olive oil, peanut oil, sunflower oil, safflower oil, and corn oil. Remember, though, that oil is only another name for liquid fat. Using oil instead of margarine or butter to fry onions or garlic will do nothing to reduce your overall intake of fat.

INGREDIENTS

One of the simplest and most beneficial changes you can make in your diet is to change from full-fat milk, cream, cheese, and yogurt to a low- or reduced-fat equivalent. Low-fat milk, for example, has all the nutritional benefits of whole milk, but only ⅓ ounce of fat per 2½ cups, compared with ¾ ounce of fat per 2½ cups in whole milk. Use skim milk to make custards and sauces and you will not notice the difference in flavor. Low-fat yogurt mixed with chopped chives is a delicious and healthy alternative to butter or sour cream.

Most vegetables are naturally low in fat and can be used to make a meal of meat or fish go further. Recent nutritional research indicates that we should all aim to eat five portions of fresh fruit and vegetables every day because they contain what are known as antioxidant vitamins, including beta carotene (which creates vitamin A in the body), and vitamins C and E. The antioxidant vitamins in vegetables are thought to help prevent a number of degenerative illnesses (including cancer, heart diseases, arthritis, and even aging of the skin) and to protect the body from the harmful effects of pollution and ultraviolet light, which can damage the body's cells. Phytochemicals, which occur naturally in plants, are thought to be instrumental in the fight against cancer.

Steaming is the best way to cook vegetables to preserve their goodness. Boiling can, for example, destroy up to three-quarters of the vitamin C present in green vegetables. If you have to boil, cook the vegetables as quickly as possible and avoid over-cooking, which also destroys the carotene.

If you have time, it is a good idea to make your own stock to use as the basis of casseroles and soups. The ready-made stocks and stock cubes that are available from stores are often high in salt and artificial flavorings. Instead, use fresh herbs and spices in the water in which vegetables have been cooked or in which dried mushrooms have been soaked. Liquids in which meat and fish of various kinds have been cooked should be saved, too. Chill the liquid in the refrigerator and you will easily be able to remove and discard the fat, which will have risen to the top of the container and solidified.

Pastas, noodles, legumes, and grains can all be used in the low-fat diet, and they are useful for bulking out dishes. Pasta is available in a wide range of shapes and patterns, and it is an excellent food for boosting your carbohydrate intake. Inadequate intake of carbohydrates can result in fatigue and poor energy levels. Whole-wheat pasta is also particularly high in fiber, which helps to speed the passage of waste material through the digestive system. Stir cooked brown rice into soups and casseroles to thicken them, or mix one part red lentils with three parts lean ground beef to make a smaller amount of meat go further. Before you buy, check that noodles and pastas have not been enriched with egg. Instead look for whole- wheat or rice varieties.

EQUIPMENT

Money spent on good quality nonstick pans and cookware will not be wasted. Not only will they directly reduce the amount of fat needed for cooking, but they will save you time because they are easier to clean. Remember to use plastic implements or wooden spoons with nonstick pans so that you do not scratch the surface.

A ridged skillet makes it possible to cook with the minimum amount of fat or oil, because the fat drips down between the ridges rather than being absorbed by the food. Woks are useful—although not essential—for stir-fries. When you are stir-frying, use the smallest possible amount of oil. Keep the heat constant and the food moving to ensure quick, even cooking. Use a nonstick wok, which will help you cut down still further on the amount of oil you need.

Use a perforated or slotted spoon to remove food from the skillet, so that cooking juices—particularly fats—are left behind. Absorbent paper towels are useful for draining surface oil and fat from food that has just been cooked, but they can also be used to mop up fat that rises to the top of a saucepan during cooking. Use plain, unpatterned paper towels so that no dye is transferred to the food.

Soups & Starters

Many favorite snacks and starters—especially those that we buy ready-prepared on supermarket shelves and in cans—are surprisingly high in fat. Next time, before you buy, think instead about making some of the appetizing recipes on the following pages—they will get your meal off to a wonderful low-fat start.

Soups are a traditional first course, but, served with crusty bread, they can also be a satisfying meal in their own right. Although it does take a little longer, consider making your own stock by using the liquid left after cooking vegetables, and the juices from fish and meat that have been used as the base of casseroles. Use a potato to thicken your soups, rather than stirring in the traditional thickener of flour and water—or, worse, flour and fat.

If you want a change from soup, try a few starters, such as a light Cheesy Ham and Celery Savory or Parsleyed Chicken and Ham Pâté served with a refreshing salad and crisp breads, or flavor-filled Spinach Cheese Molds.

Chicken & Asparagus Soup

This light, clear soup has a delicate flavor of asparagus and herbs. Use a good quality stock for best results.

Serves 4

CALORIES PER SERVING: 236 • FAT CONTENT PER SERVING: 2.9 G

INGREDIENTS

8 ounces fresh asparagus
$3^3/_4$ cups fresh chicken stock
$^2/_3$ cup dry white wine

1 sprig each fresh parsley, dill,
  and tarragon
1 garlic clove
$^1/_3$ cup vermicelli rice noodles

12 ounces lean cooked chicken, finely
  shredded
salt and white pepper
1 small leek, shredded, to garnish

1 Wash the asparagus and trim away the woody ends. Cut each spear into pieces about 1½ inches long.

2 Pour the stock and wine into a large saucepan and bring to a boil.

3 Wash the herbs and tie them with clean string. Peel the garlic clove and add, with the herbs, to the saucepan, together with the asparagus and noodles. Cover and simmer for 5 minutes.

4 Stir in the chicken and plenty of seasoning. Simmer gently for a further 3–4 minutes until heated through.

5 Trim the leek, slice it down the center, and wash under running water to remove any dirt. Shake dry and shred finely.

6 Remove the herbs and garlic from the pan and discard. Ladle the soup into warm bowls, sprinkle with shredded leek, and serve at once.

VARIATION

You can use any of your favorite herbs in this recipe, but choose those with a subtle flavor so that they do not overpower the asparagus. Small, tender asparagus spears give the best results and flavor.

COOK'S TIP

Rice noodles contain no fat and are an ideal substitute for egg noodles.

Beef, Water Chestnut, & Rice Soup

Strips of tender lean beef are combined with crisp water chestnuts and cooked rice in a tasty beef broth with a tang of orange.

Serves 4

CALORIES PER SERVING: 205 • FAT CONTENT PER SERVING: 4.5 G

INGREDIENTS

12 ounces lean beef (such as rump or sirloin)
4 cups fresh beef stock
cinnamon stick, broken
2 star anise
2 tbsp dark soy sauce
2 tbsp dry sherry

3 tbsp tomato paste
4 ounce can water chestnuts, drained and sliced
3 cups cooked white rice
1 tsp zested orange rind
6 tbsp orange juice
salt and pepper

TO GARNISH:
strips of orange rind
2 tbsp snipped chives

1 Using a sharp knife, carefully trim away any fat from the beef. Cut the beef into thin strips and then place into a large saucepan.

2 Add the stock, cinnamon, star anise, soy sauce, sherry, tomato paste, and water chestnuts. Bring to a boil, skimming away any surface scum with a flat ladle. Cover the pan and simmer gently for about 20 minutes or until the beef is tender.

3 Skim the soup with a flat ladle again to remove any scum. Remove and discard the cinnamon and star anise and blot the surface with absorbent paper towels to remove any fat.

4 Stir in the rice, orange rind, and juice. Adjust the seasoning if necessary. Heat through for 2–3 minutes before ladling into warm bowls. Serve garnished with strips of orange rind and snipped chives.

VARIATION

Omit the rice for a lighter soup that is an ideal starter for a Chinese meal of many courses. For a more substantial soup that would be a meal in its own right, add diced vegetables such as carrot, bell pepper, corn, or zucchini.

Winter Beef & Vegetable Soup

This comforting broth is perfect for a cold day and is sure to warm you up.

Serves 4

CALORIES PER SERVING: 161 • FAT CONTENT PER SERVING: 3.3 G

INGREDIENTS

1/3 cup pearl barley	1 leek, shredded	2 tbsp fresh parsley, chopped,
5 cups fresh beef stock	1 medium onion, chopped	to garnish
1 tsp dried mixed herbs	2 celery stalks, sliced	crusty bread, to serve
8 ounces lean rump or sirloin beef	salt and pepper	
1 large carrot, diced		

1 Place the pearl barley in a large saucepan. Pour in the stock and add the mixed herbs. Bring to a boil, cover, and simmer for 10 minutes.

2 Meanwhile, trim any fat from the beef and cut the meat into thin strips.

3 Skim away any scum that has risen to the top of the stock with a flat ladle.

4 Add the beef, carrot, leek, onion, and celery to the pan.

Bring back to a boil, cover, and simmer for about 20 minutes or until the meat and vegetables are just tender.

5 Skim away any remaining scum that has risen to the top of the soup with a flat ladle. Blot the surface with absorbent paper towels to remove any fat. Adjust the seasoning according to taste.

6 Ladle the soup into warm bowls and sprinkle with freshly chopped parsley. Serve accompanied with crusty bread.

VARIATION

This soup is just as delicious made with lean lamb or pork tenderloin. A vegetarian version can be made by omitting the beef and beef stock and using vegetable stock instead. Just before serving, stir in 6 ounces fresh bean curd, drained and diced. An even more substantial soup can be made by adding other root vegetables, such as rutabaga or turnip, instead of, or as well as, the carrot.

Mediterranean-style Fish Soup

Juicy chunks of fish and sumptuous shellfish are cooked in a flavorsome tomato, herb, and wine stock. Serve with toasted bread rubbed with garlic.

Serves 4

CALORIES PER SERVING: 270 • FAT CONTENT PER SERVING: 5.3 G

INGREDIENTS

1 tbsp olive oil
1 large onion, chopped
2 garlic cloves, finely chopped
1³/₄ cups fresh fish stock
²/₃ cup dry white wine
1 bay leaf
1 sprig each fresh thyme, rosemary, and oregano

1 pound firm white fish fillets (such as cod, monkfish or halibut), skinned and cut into 1-inch cubes
1 pound fresh mussels, prepared
14 ounce can chopped tomatoes
8 ounces peeled shrimp, thawed if frozen
salt and pepper
sprigs of thyme, to garnish

TO SERVE:
lemon wedges
4 slices toasted French bread, rubbed with cut garlic clove

1 Heat the oil in a large saucepan and gently sauté the onion and garlic for 2–3 minutes, until just softened.

2 Pour in the stock and wine and bring to a boil. Tie the bay leaf and herbs together with clean string and add to the saucepan, together with the fish and mussels. Stir well, cover, and simmer for 5 minutes.

3 Stir in the tomatoes and shrimp and continue to cook for a further 3–4 minutes, until piping hot and the fish is cooked through.

4 Discard the herbs and any mussels that have not opened. Season to taste, then ladle into warm bowls. Garnish with sprigs of fresh thyme and serve with lemon wedges and toasted bread.

COOK'S TIP

Traditionally, the toasted bread is placed at the bottom of the bowl and the soup spooned over the top. For convenience, use prepared, cooked shellfish mixes, instead of fresh fish. Simply add to the soup with the tomatoes in step 3.

Tuscan Bean & Vegetable Soup

This thick, satisfying blend of beans and diced vegetables in a rich red wine and tomato stock, based on an Italian favorite, makes an ideal simple supper.

Serves 4

CALORIES PER SERVING: 156 • FAT CONTENT PER SERVING: 1.5 G

INGREDIENTS

1 medium onion, chopped
1 garlic clove, finely chopped
2 celery stalks, sliced
1 large carrot, diced
14 ounce can chopped tomatoes
2/3 cup Italian dry
   red wine

5 cups fresh vegetable stock
1 tsp dried oregano
15 ounce can mixed beans
   and legumes
2 medium zucchini, diced
1 tbsp tomato paste
salt and pepper

TO SERVE:
low-fat pesto sauce (see page 146)
crusty bread

1 Place the prepared onion, garlic, celery, and carrot in a large saucepan. Stir in the tomatoes, red wine, vegetable stock, and oregano.

2 Bring the vegetable mixture to a boil, cover the pan, and simmer for about 15 minutes. Stir the beans and zucchini into the mixture, and continue to cook, uncovered, for a further 5 minutes.

3 Add the tomato paste and season well with salt and pepper to taste. Then heat through, stirring occasionally, for a further 2–3 minutes, but do not allow the mixture to boil again.

4 Ladle the soup into warm bowls and serve with a spoonful of low-fat pesto (see page 146) on each portion and accompanied with lots of fresh crusty bread.

VARIATION

For a more substantial soup, add 12 ounces diced lean cooked chicken or turkey with the tomato paste in step 3.

Lentil, Pasta, & Vegetable Soup

*Packed with the flavor of garlic, this soup is a filling supper
dish when it is served with crusty bread and a crisp salad.*

Serves 4

CALORIES PER SERVING: 378 • FAT CONTENT PER SERVING: 4.9 G

INGREDIENTS

1 tbsp olive oil
1 medium onion, chopped
4 garlic cloves, finely chopped
12 ounces carrots, sliced
1 celery stalk, sliced
1¼ cups red lentils

2½ cups fresh vegetable stock
3 cups boiling water
1 cup dried pasta

⅔ cup natural low-fat unsweetened
   yogurt, plus extra to serve
salt and pepper
2 tbsp fresh parsley, chopped,
   to garnish

1 Heat the oil in a large
saucepan and gently sauté the
prepared onion, garlic, carrot, and
celery, stirring gently, for
5 minutes until the vegetables
begin to soften.

2 Add the lentils, stock, and
boiling water. Season well,
stir and bring back to a boil.
Simmer, uncovered, for
15 minutes until the lentils are
completely tender. Allow to cool
for 10 minutes.

3 Meanwhile, bring another
saucepan of water to a boil
and cook the pasta according to the
instructions on the packet. Drain
well and set aside.

4 Place the soup in a blender
and process until smooth.
Return to a saucepan and add the
pasta. Bring back to a simmer and
heat for 2–3 minutes, until piping
hot. Remove from the heat and stir
in the yogurt. Adjust the seasoning
if necessary.

5 Serve sprinkled with freshly
ground black pepper and
chopped parsley and with extra
yogurt if wished.

COOK'S TIP

*Avoid boiling the soup once the
yogurt has been added. Otherwise it
will separate and become watery,
spoiling the appearance of the soup.*

Creamy Corn Soup

Based on a traditional chowder recipe, this filling combination of tender corn kernels and a creamy stock is extra delicious with lean diced ham sprinkled on top.

Serves 4

CALORIES PER SERVING: 346 • FAT CONTENT PER SERVING: 2.4 G

INGREDIENTS

1 large onion, chopped
1 large potato, peeled and diced
4 cups skim milk
1 bay leaf
$\frac{1}{2}$ tsp ground nutmeg

1 pound canned corn kernels or
 frozen, drained or thawed
1 tbsp cornstarch
3 tbsp cold water
4 tbsp natural low-fat
 unsweetened yogurt

salt and pepper

TO GARNISH:
$3\frac{1}{2}$ ounces lean ham, diced
2 tbsp snipped fresh chives

1 Place the onion and potato in a large saucepan and pour in the milk. Add the bay leaf, nutmeg, and half the corn. Bring to a boil, cover, and simmer gently for 15 minutes, until the potato is softened. Stir the soup occasionally and keep the heat low so that the milk does not burn on the bottom of the pan.

2 Discard the bay leaf and leave the liquid to cool for 10 minutes. Transfer to a blender and process briefly. Alternatively, rub through a strainer.

3 Pour the smooth liquid into a saucepan. Blend the cornstarch with the cold water to make a paste and stir it into the soup.

4 Bring the soup back to a boil, stirring until it thickens, and add the remaining corn. Heat through for 2–3 minutes until piping hot.

5 Remove from the heat and season with salt and pepper. Stir in the yogurt. Ladle the soup into warm bowls and serve sprinkled with the diced ham and snipped chives.

VARIATION

For a more substantial soup, add 8 ounces flaked white crabmeat or peeled, cooked shrimp in step 4.

Tomato & Red Bell Pepper Soup

*Sweet red bell peppers and tangy tomatoes are blended together
in a smooth vegetable soup that makes a perfect starter or light lunch.*

Serves 4

CALORIES PER SERVING: 93 • FAT CONTENT PER SERVING: 1 G

INGREDIENTS

2 large red bell peppers
1 large onion, chopped
2 celery stalks, trimmed and chopped
1 garlic clove, crushed

$2^1/_2$ cups fresh vegetable stock
2 bay leaves
2 x 14 ounce cans plum tomatoes
salt and pepper

2 scallions, finely shredded,
 to garnish
crusty bread, to serve

1 Preheat the broiler. Halve and seed the bell peppers, arrange them on the broiler rack and cook, turning occasionally, for 8–10 minutes until softened and charred.

2 Leave to cool slightly, then carefully peel off the charred skin. Reserving a small piece for garnish, chop the bell pepper flesh and place in a large saucepan.

3 Mix in the onion, celery, and garlic. Add the stock and the bay leaves. Bring to a boil, cover, and simmer for 15 minutes. Remove from the heat.

4 Stir in the tomatoes and transfer to a blender. Process for a few seconds until smooth. Return to the saucepan.

5 Season with salt and pepper to taste and heat for 3–4 minutes until piping hot. Ladle the soup into warm bowls and garnish with the reserved bell pepper cut into strips and the scallion floating on the top. Serve with lots of fresh crusty bread.

COOK'S TIP

If you prefer a coarser, more robust soup, lightly mash the tomatoes with a wooden spoon and omit the blending process in step 4.

Carrot, Apple, & Celery Soup

This fresh-tasting soup is ideal as a light starter. Use your favorite eating apple rather than a cooking variety, which will give too tart a flavor.

Serves 4

CALORIES PER SERVING: 150 • FAT CONTENT PER SERVING: 1.4 G

INGREDIENTS

2 pounds carrots, finely diced
1 medium onion, chopped
3 celery stalks, trimmed and diced
4 cups fresh vegetable stock

3 medium-size eating
  apples
2 tbsp tomato paste
1 bay leaf
2 tsp superfine sugar

¹/₄ large lemon
salt and pepper
celery leaves, washed and shredded,
  to garnish

1 Place the prepared carrots, onion, and celery in a large saucepan and add the stock. Bring to a boil, cover and simmer for 10 minutes.

2 Meanwhile, peel, core, and dice 2 of the apples. Add the pieces of apple, tomato paste, bay leaf, and superfine sugar to the saucepan and bring to a boil. Reduce the heat, half cover the pan, and allow to simmer for 20 minutes. Remove and discard the bay leaf.

3 Meanwhile, wash, core, and cut the remaining apple into thin slices, leaving on the skin. Place the apple slices in a small saucepan and squeeze in the lemon juice. Heat gently and simmer for 1–2 minutes, until tender. Drain and set aside.

4 Place the carrot and apple mixture in a blender or food processor and blend until smooth. Alternatively, press the mixture through a strainer with the back of a wooden spoon.

5 Gently reheat the soup if necessary and season with salt and pepper to taste. Ladle the soup into warm bowls and serve topped with the reserved apple slices and shredded celery leaves.

COOK'S TIP

Soaking light colored fruit in lemon juice helps to prevent it from turning brown.

Chilled Piquant Shrimp & Cucumber Soup

Serve this soup over ice on a warm summer day as a refreshing starter.
It has the fresh tang of yogurt and a dash of spice from the Tabasco sauce.

Serves 4

CALORIES PER SERVING: 104 • FAT CONTENT PER SERVING: 1 G

INGREDIENTS

1 cucumber, peeled and diced
1²/₃ cups fresh fish stock, chilled
²/₃ cup tomato juice
1²/₃ cup low-fat unsweetened yogurt
4¹/₂ ounces peeled shrimp, thawed
  if frozen, roughly chopped
few drops Tabasco sauce

1 tbsp fresh mint, chopped
salt and white pepper
ice cubes, to serve

TO GARNISH:
sprigs of mint
cucumber slices
whole peeled shrimp

1 Place the diced cucumber in a blender or food processor and work for a few seconds until a smooth purée is formed. Alternatively, chop the cucumber finely and push through a strainer.

2 Transfer the cucumber to a bowl. Stir in the stock, tomato juice, yogurt, and shrimp, and mix well. Add the Tabasco sauce and season to taste.

3 Stir in the chopped mint, cover, and chill for at least 2 hours.

4 Ladle the soup into glass bowls and add a few ice cubes. Serve garnished with mint, cucumber slices, and whole shrimp.

VARIATION

Instead of shrimp, add white crabmeat or cooked ground chicken. For a vegetarian version of this soup, omit the shrimp, and add an extra 4¹/₂ ounces finely diced cucumber. Use fresh vegetable stock instead of fish stock.

Rosy Melon & Strawberries

The combination of sweet melon and strawberries macerated in rosé wine and a hint of rosewater is a delightful start to a special meal.

Serves 4

CALORIES PER SERVING: 83 • FAT CONTENT PER SERVING: 0.2 G

INGREDIENTS

1/4 honeydew melon
1/2 Charentais or Cantaloupe melon
2/3 cup rosé wine

2–3 tsp rosewater
6 ounces small strawberries, washed and hulled

rose petals, to garnish

1 Scoop out the seeds from both melons with a spoon. Then carefully remove the skin, taking care not to remove too much flesh.

2 Cut the melon flesh into thin strips and place in a bowl. Pour in the wine and sufficient rosewater to taste. Mix together gently, cover, and chill in the refrigerator for at least 2 hours.

3 Halve the strawberries and carefully mix into the melon. Allow the melon and strawberries

to stand at room temperature for about 15 minutes for the flavors to develop fully.

4 Arrange the melon and strawberries on individual serving plates and serve sprinkled with a few rose petals.

COOK'S TIP

Rosewater is generally available from large pharmacies and leading supermarkets, as well as from more specialty food suppliers.

COOK'S TIP

It does not matter whether the rosé wine is sweet or dry—although sweet wine contains more calories. Experiment with different types of melon. Varieties such as "Sweet Dream" have whitish-green flesh, while Charentais melons, which have orange flesh, are fragrant and go better with a dry wine. If you wish, soak the strawberries in the wine with the melon, but always allow the fruit to return to room temperature before serving.

Italian Platter

This popular hors d'oeuvre usually consists of vegetables soaked in olive oil and accompanied with rich, creamy cheeses. Try this equally good low-fat version.

Serves 4

CALORIES PER SERVING: 175 • FAT CONTENT PER SERVING: 7.6 G

INGREDIENTS

4¹/₂ ounces reduced-fat mozzarella
   cheese, drained
2 ounces lean prosciutto
14 ounce can artichoke
   hearts, drained
4 ripe figs
1 small mango

plain bread sticks,
   to serve

FOR THE DRESSING:
1 small orange
1 tbsp sieved tomatoes
1 tsp wholegrain mustard

4 tbsp low-fat unsweetened yogurt
fresh basil leaves
salt and pepper

1 Cut the cheese into 12 sticks, 2½ inches long. Remove the fat from the ham and slice the meat into 12 strips.

2 Carefully wrap a strip of ham around each stick of cheese and arrange them neatly on a serving platter.

3 Halve the artichoke hearts and cut the figs into quarters. Arrange them on the serving platter in groups.

4 Peel the mango, then slice it down each side of the large, flat central pit. Slice the flesh into strips and arrange them so that they form a fan shape on the serving platter.

5 To make the dressing, pare the rind from half the orange using a vegetable peeler. Cut the rind into small strips and place them in a bowl. Extract the juice from the orange and add it to the bowl containing the rind.

6 Add the sieved tomatoes, mustard, yogurt, and seasoning to the bowl and mix together. Shred the basil leaves and mix them into the dressing.

7 Spoon the dressing into a small dish and serve with the Italian Platter, accompanied with bread sticks.

Breakfast Muffins

*Try this filling breakfast or brunch idea for a good start to the day—a toasted
English muffin, topped with lean bacon, broiled tomato, mushrooms, and a poached egg.*

Serves 4

CALORIES PER SERVING: 270 • FAT CONTENT PER SERVING: 12.3 G

INGREDIENTS

2 whole-wheat English muffins
8 slices lean bacon

4 medium eggs
2 large tomatoes
2 large flat mushrooms

4 tbsp fresh vegetable stock
salt and pepper
1 small bunch fresh chives, snipped,
  to garnish

1 Preheat the broiler. Cut the muffins in half and lightly toast them for 1–2 minutes on the open side. Set aside and keep warm.

2 Trim off all visible fat from the bacon and broil for 2–3 minutes on each side until cooked through. Drain on absorbent paper towels and keep warm.

3 Place 4 egg-poaching rings in a skillet and pour in enough water to cover the base of the pan. Bring to a boil and reduce the heat to a simmer. Carefully break one egg into each ring and poach gently for 5–6 minutes until set.

4 Meanwhile, cut the tomatoes into 8 thick slices and arrange on a piece of kitchen foil on the broiler rack. Broil for 2–3 minutes, until just cooked. Season to taste.

5 Peel and thickly slice the mushrooms. Place in a saucepan with the stock, bring to a boil, cover, and simmer for 4–5 minutes until cooked. Drain thoroughly, set aside and keep warm until ready to serve.

6 To serve, arrange the tomato and mushroom slices on the toasted muffins and top each with 2 slices of bacon. Carefully arrange an egg on top of each and sprinkle with a little pepper. Garnish with snipped fresh chives and serve at once.

VARIATION

Omit the bacon for a vegetarian version and use more tomatoes and mushrooms instead. Alternatively, include a broiled low-fat tofu or soy protein burger.

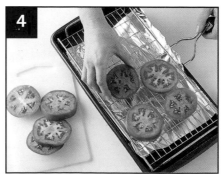

Cheesy Ham & Celery Savory

*Crisp celery wrapped in lean ham, topped with a light crust of
cheese and scallions, makes a delicious light lunch.*

Serves 4

CALORIES PER SERVING: 155 • FAT CONTENT PER SERVING: 6.9 G

INGREDIENTS

4 celery stalks, with leaves
12 thin slices of lean ham
1 bunch scallions
6 ounces low-fat soft cheese with
   garlic and herbs

6 tbsp low-fat unsweetened yogurt
4 tbsp Parmesan cheese,
   freshly grated
celery salt and pepper

TO SERVE:
tomato salad
crusty bread

1 Wash the celery, remove the leaves and reserve (if desired). Slice the celery stalks into 3 equal portions.

2 Cut any visible fat off the ham and lay the slices on a chopping board. Place a piece of celery on each piece of ham and roll up. Place 3 ham and celery rolls in each of 4 small, heatproof dishes.

3 Trim the scallions, then finely shred both the white and green parts. Sprinkle the shredded scallions over the ham and celery rolls and season with celery salt and pepper.

4 Mix together the soft cheese and yogurt and spoon over the ham and celery rolls.

5 Preheat the broiler. Sprinkle each portion with 1 tbsp grated Parmesan cheese and broil for 6–7 minutes until hot and the cheese has formed a crust. If the cheese starts to brown too quickly, lower the broiler setting slightly.

6 Serve immediately, garnished with chopped celery leaves (if using) and accompanied with a tomato salad and lots of fresh crusty bread.

COOK'S TIP

Parmesan is useful in low-fat recipes because its intense flavor means you need to use only a small amount.

Parsleyed Chicken & Ham Pâté

*Pâté is easy to make at home, and this combination of lean chicken
and ham mixed with herbs is especially straightforward.*

Serves 4

CALORIES PER SERVING: 132 • FAT CONTENT PER SERVING: 1.8 G

INGREDIENTS

8 ounces lean, skinless
  chicken, cooked
3¹/₂ ounces lean ham, trimmed
small bunch fresh parsley
1 tsp lime rind, grated
2 tbsp lime juice

1 garlic clove, peeled
¹/₂ cup low-fat unsweetened yogurt
salt and pepper
1 tsp lime zest, to garnish

TO SERVE:
wedges of lime
crisp bread
salad greens

1 Dice the chicken and ham
and place in a blender or food
processor. Add the parsley, lime
rind and juice, and garlic and
process well until finely ground.
Alternatively, finely chop the
chicken, ham, parsley, and garlic
and place in a bowl. Mix gently
with the lime rind and juice.

2 Transfer the mixture to a
bowl and mix in the yogurt.
Season with salt and pepper to
taste, cover, and set aside to chill

in the refrigerator for about
30 minutes.

3 Pile the pâté into individual
serving dishes and garnish
with lime zest. Serve the pâtés
with lime wedges, crisp bread, and
fresh salad greens.

VARIATION

*This pâté can be made
equally successfully with other
kinds of ground, lean, cooked meat,
such as turkey, beef, and pork.
Alternatively, replace the chicken
and ham with peeled shrimp
and/or white crabmeat or with
canned tuna in brine, drained.
Remember that removing the skin
from poultry reduces the fat
content of any dish.*

Spinach Cheese Molds

These flavor-packed little molds are a perfect starter or a tasty light lunch. Serve them with warm pita bread.

Serves 4

CALORIES PER SERVING: 64 • FAT CONTENT PER SERVING: 0.2 G

INGREDIENTS

3¹/₂ ounces fresh spinach leaves
10¹/₂ ounces skim milk soft cheese
2 garlic cloves, crushed

sprigs of fresh parsley, tarragon, and chives, finely chopped
salt and pepper

TO SERVE:
salad greens and fresh herbs
pita bread

1 Trim the stalks from the spinach leaves and rinse the leaves under running water. Pack the leaves into a saucepan while still wet, cover, and cook for 3–4 minutes until wilted—they will cook in the steam from the wet leaves (do not overcook). Drain well and pat dry with absorbent paper towels.

2 Base-line 4 small pudding basins or individual ramekin dishes with baking parchment. Line the basins or ramekins with spinach leaves so that the leaves overhang the edges if they are large enough to do so.

3 Place the cheese in a bowl and add the garlic and herbs. Mix together thoroughly and season to taste.

4 Spoon the cheese and herb mixture into the basins or ramekins and pull over the overlapping spinach to cover the cheese, or lay extra leaves to cover the top. Place a baking paper round on top of each dish and weigh down with a 4 ounce weight. Chill in the refrigerator for 1 hour.

5 Remove the weights and peel off the paper. Loosen the molds gently by running a small spatula around the edges of each dish and turn them onto individual serving plates.

6 Serve with a mixture of salad greens and fresh herbs, and warm pita bread.

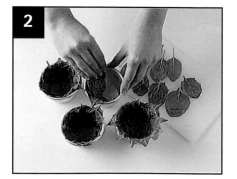

Soufflé Omelet

The mouthwatering filling of sweet cherry tomatoes, mushrooms, and peppery arugula leaves is a wonderful contrast to the light fluffy omelets, which have to be cooked one by one.

Serves 4

CALORIES PER SERVING: 141 • FAT CONTENT PER SERVING: 9.7 G

INGREDIENTS

6 ounces cherry tomatoes
8 ounces mixed mushrooms (such as
   button, chestnut, shiitake, oyster)
4 tbsp fresh vegetable stock

small bunch fresh thyme
4 medium eggs, separated
4 medium egg whites
4 tsp olive oil

1 ounce arugula leaves
salt and pepper
fresh thyme sprigs, to garnish

1 Halve the tomatoes and place them in a saucepan. Wipe the mushrooms with paper towels, trim if necessary, and slice if large. Place in the saucepan.

2 Add the stock and thyme to the pan. Bring to a boil, cover, and simmer for 5–6 minutes until tender. Drain, remove the thyme and discard, and keep the mixture warm.

3 Meanwhile, whisk the egg yolks with 8 tbsp water until frothy. In a clean, greasefree bowl, mix the 8 egg whites until stiff and dry.

4 Spoon the egg yolk mixture into the egg whites and, using a metal spoon, fold the whites and yolks into each other until well mixed. Take care not to knock out too much of the air.

5 For each omelet, brush a small omelet pan with 1 tsp oil and heat until hot. Pour in a quarter of the egg mixture and cook for 4–5 minutes, until the mixture has set.

6 Preheat the broiler and finish cooking the omelet for 2–3 minutes.

7 Transfer the omelet to a warm serving plate. Fill the omelet with a a few arugula leaves, and a quarter of the mushroom and tomato mixture. Flip over the top of the omelet, garnish with sprigs of thyme, and serve.

Broiled Rice & Tuna Bell Peppers

Broiled mixed sweet bell peppers are filled with tender tuna, corn,
nutty brown and wild rice, and grated, reduced-fat Cheddar cheese.

Serves 4

CALORIES PER SERVING: 383 • FAT CONTENT PER SERVING: 6.8 G

INGREDIENTS

^{1}/3 cup wild rice
^{1}/3 cup brown rice
4 assorted medium bell peppers
7 ounce can tuna fish in brine,
 drained and flaked

11^1/2 ounce can corn kernels (with no
 added sugar or salt), drained
3^1/2 ounces reduced-fat Cheddar
 cheese, grated
1 bunch fresh basil leaves, shredded
2 tbsp dry white breadcrumbs

1 tbsp Parmesan cheese,
 freshly grated
salt and pepper
fresh basil leaves, to garnish
crisp salad, to serve

1 Place the 2 rices in different saucepans, cover with water, and cook according to the instructions on the packet. Drain well.

2 Meanwhile, preheat the broiler. Halve the bell peppers, remove the seeds and stalks, and arrange the peppers on the broiler rack, cut side down. Cook for 5 minutes, turn over, and cook for 4–5 minutes.

3 Transfer the cooked rice to a mixing bowl and add the flaked tuna and drained corn. Gently fold in the grated cheese. Mix in the basil leaves and season to taste.

4 Divide the tuna and rice mixture into 8 equal portions. Pile each portion into each cooked bell pepper half. Mix together the breadcrumbs and Parmesan cheese and sprinkle over each bell pepper.

5 Place the bell peppers back under the broiler for 4–5 minutes, until hot and golden-brown. Serve immediately, garnished with fresh basil leaves and accompanied with a fresh, crisp salad.

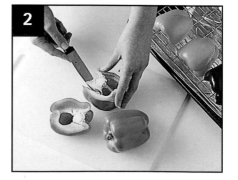

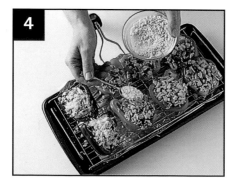

Baked Potatoes with a Spicy Filling

*Crisp, twice-baked potatoes are partnered with an unusual filling of the
Middle Eastern flavors of garbanzo beans, cumin, and coriander.*

Serves 4

CALORIES PER SERVING: 354 • FAT CONTENT PER SERVING: 5.9 G

INGREDIENTS

4 baking potatoes, each about
  $10^1/_2$ ounces
1 tbsp vegetable oil
$15^1/_2$ ounce can garbanzo
  beans, drained

1 tsp ground coriander
1 tsp ground cumin
4 tbsp fresh cilantro, chopped
$^2/_3$ cup low-fat unsweetened yogurt

salt and pepper
salad, to serve

1 Preheat the oven to 400°F. Scrub the potatoes and pat them dry on absorbent paper towels. Prick them all over with a fork, brush with oil, and season to taste with salt and pepper.

2 Place the potatoes on a cookie sheet and bake for 1–1¼ hours, or until cooked through. Cool for 10 minutes.

3 Meanwhile, mash the garbanzo beans with a fork or potato masher. Stir in the spices and half the chopped cilantro. Cover and set aside.

4 Halve the cooked potatoes and scoop the flesh into a bowl, keeping the shells intact. Mash the flesh until smooth and gently mix into the garbanzo bean mixture with the yogurt. Season well with salt and pepper.

5 Place the potato shells on a cookie sheet and fill with the potato and garbanzo bean mixture. Return the potatoes to the oven and bake for 10–15 minutes, until heated through.

6 Serve sprinkled with the remaining chopped cilantro and a fresh salad made of chopped tomato, cucumber, cilantro, and red onion.

COOK'S TIP

For an even lower fat version of this recipe, bake the potatoes without oiling them first.

Spinach Crêpes with Curried Crab

Homemade crêpes are delicious and can be served with a variety of fillings. Here, white crabmeat is lightly flavored with curry spices and tossed in a low-fat dressing.

Serves 4

CALORIES PER SERVING: 259 • FAT CONTENT PER SERVING: 5.9 G

INGREDIENTS

4 ounces buckwheat flour
1 large egg, beaten
1¼ cups skim milk
4½ ounces frozen spinach, thawed,
   well-drained and chopped
2 tsp vegetable oil

FOR THE FILLING:
12 ounces white crabmeat
1 tsp mild curry powder
1 tbsp mango chutney
1 tbsp reduced-calorie mayonnaise
2 tbsp low-fat unsweetened yogurt
2 tbsp fresh cilantro, chopped

TO SERVE:
salad greens
lemon wedges

1 Sift the flour into a bowl and remove any husks that remain in the strainer.

2 Make a well in the center of the flour and add the egg. Gradually whisk in the milk, then blend in the spinach. Transfer the batter to a pitcher and allow to stand for 30 minutes.

3 To make the filling, mix together all the ingredients, except the cilantro, in a bowl, cover, and chill until required.

4 Whisk the batter. Brush a small crêpe pan with a little oil, heat until hot, and pour in enough batter to cover the base thinly. Cook for 1–2 minutes until set, turn over and cook for 1 minute until golden. Transfer to a warmed plate. Repeat to make 8 pancakes, layering them on the plate with baking parchment.

5 Stir the cilantro into the crab mixture. Fold each pancake into quarters. Open one fold and fill with the crab mixture. Serve warm, with salad greens and lemon wedges.

VARIATION

Try lean diced chicken in a light white sauce or peeled shrimp instead of the crab.

Meat & Poultry

The increased interest in healthy eating means that most supermarkets and butchers now offer special cuts of lean meat. Although they are often slightly more expensive than standard cuts, it is worth buying this meat and spending a little extra time cooking it carefully to enhance the flavor. You will not need to buy as much if you combine the meat with thoughtfully chosen and prepared vegetables.

Look for packs of low- or reduced-fat ground meat in your local supermarket, and include it in burgers or serve it in a flavor-filled sauce with rice or your favorite pasta.

Cut any visible fat from beef and pork before you cook it. Chicken and turkey are lower in fat than red meats, and you can make them even healthier by removing the skin. Duck is a rich meat with a distinctive flavor, and you need only a small amount to create apparently extravagant, flavorful dishes that are healthy, too.

Pan-cooked Pork with Fennel & Aniseed

Lean pork chops, stuffed with an aniseed and orange filling, are pan-cooked with fennel in an aniseed-flavored sweet sauce.

Serves 4

CALORIES PER SERVING: 242 • FAT CONTENT PER SERVING: 6.4 G

INGREDIENTS

4 lean pork chops, 4$^{1}/_{2}$ ounces each
$^{1}/_{3}$ cup brown rice, cooked
1 tsp orange rind, grated
4 scallions, trimmed and
   finely chopped
$^{1}/_{2}$ tsp aniseed

1 tbsp olive oil
1 fennel bulb, trimmed and
   thinly sliced
2 cups unsweetened orange juice
1 tbsp cornstarch
2 tbsp Pernod

salt and pepper
fennel fronds, to garnish
cooked vegetables, to serve

1 Trim away any excess fat from the pork chops. Using a small, sharp knife, make a slit in the center of each chop to create a pocket.

2 Mix the rice, orange rind, scallions, seasoning, and aniseed together in a bowl. Press the mixture into the pocket of each chop, then press gently to seal.

3 Heat the oil in a skillet and fry the pork chops on each side for 2–3 minutes, until golden.

4 Add the sliced fennel and orange juice to the skillet, bring to a boil and simmer for 15–20 minutes until the meat is tender and cooked through. Remove the pork and fennel with a slotted spoon and transfer to a serving plate.

5 Blend the cornstarch and Pernod together in a small bowl. Add the cornstarch mixture to the pan and stir into the pan juices. Cook for 2–3 minutes, stirring, until the sauce thickens.

6 Pour the Pernod sauce over the pork chops, garnish with fennel fronds, and serve with a selection of cooked vegetables, if you wish.

Pork Stroganoff

Tender, lean pork, cooked in a rich tomato sauce with mushrooms and a green bell pepper, is flavored with the extra tang of unsweetened yogurt.

Serves 4

CALORIES PER SERVING: 197 • FAT CONTENT PER SERVING: 7 G

INGREDIENTS

12 ounces lean pork tenderloin
1 tbsp vegetable oil
1 medium onion, chopped
2 garlic cloves, crushed
1 ounce all purpose flour
2 tbsp tomato paste

$1^3/_4$ cups fresh chicken or
   vegetable stock
$4^1/_2$ ounces button
   mushrooms, sliced
1 large green bell pepper, seeded
   and diced
$^1/_2$ tsp ground nutmeg

4 tbsp low-fat unsweetened yogurt,
   plus extra to serve
salt and pepper
white rice, freshly boiled, to serve
ground nutmeg, to garnish

1 Trim away any excess fat and silver skin from the pork, then cut the meat into slices ½ inch thick.

2 Heat the oil in a large pan and gently fry the pork, onion, and garlic for 4–5 minutes until lightly browned.

3 Stir in the flour and tomato paste, pour in the stock, and stir to mix thoroughly.

4 Add the mushrooms, bell pepper, seasoning, and nutmeg. Bring to a boil, cover, and simmer for 20 minutes, until the pork is tender and cooked through.

5 Remove the saucepan from the heat and stir in the yogurt.

6 Serve the pork and sauce on a bed of rice with an extra spoonful of yogurt, and garnish with a dusting of ground nutmeg.

COOK'S TIP

You can buy ready-made meat, vegetable, and fish stocks from leading supermarkets. Although more expensive, they are better nutritionally than stock cubes, which are high in salt and artificial flavorings. Homemade stock is best of all.

Pan-cooked Pork Medallions with Apples & Cider

These lean and tender cuts of meat are thick slices cut from the tenderloin. In this dish they are perfectly complemented by eating apples and hard cider.

Serves 4

CALORIES PER SERVING: 192 • FAT CONTENT PER SERVING: 5.7 G

INGREDIENTS

8 lean pork medallions, about
  1^3/4 ounces each
2 tsp vegetable oil
1 medium onion, finely sliced
1 tsp superfine sugar

1 tsp dried sage
^{2}/3 cup hard cider
^{2}/3 cup fresh chicken or
  vegetable stock
1 green-skinned apple

1 red-skinned apple
1 tbsp lemon juice
salt and pepper
fresh sage leaves, to garnish
freshly cooked vegetables, to serve

1 Discard the string from the pork and trim away any excess fat. Re-tie with clean string and set aside.

2 Heat the oil in a skillet and gently sauté the onion for 5 minutes, until softened. Add the sugar and cook for 3–4 minutes until golden.

3 Add the pork to the pan and cook for 2 minutes on each side, until browned. Add the sage, cider, and stock. Bring to a boil and then simmer for 20 minutes.

4 Meanwhile, core and cut each apple into 8 wedges. Toss the apple wedges in lemon juice so that they do not turn brown.

5 Add the apples to the pork and mix gently. Season and cook for a further 3–4 minutes, until tender.

6 Remove the string from the pork and serve immediately, garnished with fresh sage and accompanied with freshly cooked vegetables.

COOK'S TIP

If pork medallions are not available, buy 14 ounces pork tenderloin and slice it into evenly-sized medallions yourself.

Red Roast Pork with Bell Peppers

In this traditional Chinese dish the pork turns "red" during cooking because it is basted in dark soy sauce. It is ideal served with sweet mixed bell peppers.

Serves 4

CALORIES PER SERVING: 282 • FAT CONTENT PER SERVING: 5 G

INGREDIENTS

1 pound lean pork tenderloin
6 tbsp dark soy sauce
2 tbsp dry sherry
1 tsp five-spice powder
2 garlic cloves, crushed

1-inch piece fresh ginger root, finely chopped
1 large red bell pepper
1 large yellow bell pepper
1 large orange bell pepper

4 tbsp superfine sugar
2 tbsp red wine vinegar

TO GARNISH:
scallions, shredded
fresh chives, snipped

1 Trim away excess fat and silver skin from the pork and place in a shallow dish.

2 Mix together the soy sauce, sherry, five-spice powder, garlic, and ginger. Spoon over the pork, cover, and marinate in the refrigerator for at least 1 hour.

3 Preheat the oven to 375°F. Drain the pork, reserving the marinade. Place the pork on a roasting rack over a roasting pan. Cook in the oven, occasionally basting with the marinade, for 1 hour or until cooked through.

4 Meanwhile, halve and seed the bell peppers. Cut each bell pepper half into 3 equal portions. Arrange them on a cookie sheet and bake alongside the pork for the last 30 minutes of cooking time.

5 Place the superfine sugar and vinegar in a small saucepan and heat gently over a low heat until the sugar has completely dissolved. Bring to a boil and simmer for 3–4 minutes, until syrupy.

6 As soon as the pork is cooked, remove from the oven and brush with the sugar syrup. Allow to stand for 5 minutes, then slice, and arrange on a warm platter with the bell peppers. Serve immediately, garnished with the scallions and freshly snipped chives.

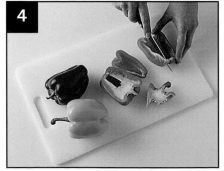

Pork with Ratatouille Sauce

*Serve this delicious combination of meat and vegetables
with baked potatoes for an appetizing supper dish.*

Serves 4

CALORIES PER SERVING: 214 • FAT CONTENT PER SERVING: 5.6 G

INGREDIENTS

4 lean, boneless pork chops, about 4$\frac{1}{2}$ ounces each	SAUCE:	3$\frac{1}{2}$ ounces button mushrooms
1 tsp dried mixed herbs	1 medium onion	14 ounce can chopped tomatoes
salt and pepper	1 garlic clove	2 tbsp tomato paste
baked potatoes, to serve	1 small green bell pepper	1 tsp dried mixed herbs
	1 small yellow bell pepper	1 tsp superfine sugar
	1 medium zucchini	

1 To make the sauce, peel and chop the onion and garlic. Seed and dice the bell peppers. Trim and dice the zucchini. Wipe and halve the mushrooms.

2 Place all of the vegetables in a saucepan and stir in the chopped tomatoes and tomato paste. Add the dried herbs, sugar, and plenty of seasoning. Bring to a boil, cover, and simmer for 20 minutes.

3 Meanwhile, preheat the broiler. Trim away any excess fat from the chops, then season on both sides, and rub in the dried mixed herbs. Cook the chops for 5 minutes, then turn over, and cook for a further 6–7 minutes until cooked through.

4 Drain the chops on absorbent paper towels and serve accompanied with the sauce and baked potatoes.

COOK'S TIP

This vegetable sauce could be served with any other broiled or baked meat or fish. It would also make an excellent alternative filling for the Spinach Crêpes on page 46.

Beef & Orange Curry

A citrusy, spicy blend of tender chunks of lean beef with the tang of orange and the warmth of Indian spices. For a well-balanced meal, serve with boiled rice and a cucumber raita.

Serves 4

CALORIES PER SERVING: 283 • FAT CONTENT PER SERVING: 10.5 G

INGREDIENTS

1 tbsp vegetable oil
8 ounces shallots, halved
2 garlic cloves, crushed
1 pound lean rump or sirloin beef, trimmed and cut into $^3/_4$ inch cubes
3 tbsp curry paste
2 cups fresh beef stock

4 medium oranges
2 tsp cornstarch
salt and pepper
2 tbsp fresh cilantro, chopped, to garnish
Basmati rice, freshly boiled, to serve

RAITA:
$^1/_2$ cucumber, finely diced
3 tbsp fresh mint, chopped
$^2/_3$ cup low-fat unsweetened yogurt

1 Heat the oil in a large saucepan. Gently fry the shallots, garlic, and the cubes of beef for 5 minutes, stirring occasionally, until the beef is evenly browned all over.

2 Blend together the curry paste and stock. Add the mixture to the beef and stir to mix thoroughly. Bring to a boil, cover, and simmer for 1 hour, or until the meat is tender.

3 Meanwhile, grate the rind of one orange. Extract the juice from the orange and from a second orange. Peel the two remaining oranges, removing as much pith as possible. Slice between each segment and remove the flesh.

4 Blend the cornstarch with the orange juice. At the end of the cooking time, stir the orange rind into the beef, along with the orange and cornstarch mixture.

Bring to a boil and simmer, stirring, for 3–4 minutes, until the sauce thickens. Season with salt and pepper to taste and stir in the orange segments.

5 To make the raita, mix the cucumber with the mint, and stir in the yogurt. Season with salt and pepper to taste.

6 Serve the curry with rice and the cucumber raita.

Pan-seared Beef with Ginger, Pineapple, & Chili

Serve these fruity, hot, and spicy steaks with noodles. Use a nonstick, ridged skillet for the best results—it will help you cook with a minimum of fat.

Serves 4

CALORIES PER SERVING: 191 • FAT CONTENT PER SERVING: 5.1 G

INGREDIENTS

4 lean beef steaks (such as rump, sirloin, or fillet), 3½ ounces each
2 tbsp ginger wine
1-inch piece fresh ginger root, finely chopped
1 garlic clove, crushed
1 tsp ground chili

1 tsp vegetable oil
red chili strips, to garnish
salt and pepper

TO SERVE:
freshly cooked noodles
2 scallions, shredded

RELISH:
8 ounces fresh pineapple
1 small red bell pepper
1 red chili
2 tbsp light soy sauce
1 piece preserved ginger in syrup, drained and chopped

1 Trim any excess fat from the beef if necessary. Using a meat mallet or covered rolling pin, pound the steaks until ½ inch thick. Season on both sides and place in a shallow dish.

2 Mix the ginger wine, ginger root, garlic, and chili and pour over the meat. Cover and chill for 30 minutes.

3 Meanwhile, make the relish. Peel and finely chop the pineapple and place it in a bowl. Halve, seed, and finely chop the bell pepper and chili. Stir into the pineapple, together with the soy sauce and preserved ginger. Cover and chill until required.

4 Brush a nonstick skillet with the oil and heat until very hot.

Drain the beef and add to the pan, pressing down to seal. Lower the heat and cook for 5 minutes. Turn the steaks over and cook for a further 5 minutes.

5 Drain the steaks on paper towels and transfer to serving plates. Garnish with chili strips, and serve with noodles, scallions, and the relish.

Beef & Tomato Gratin

A satisfying bake of lean ground beef, zucchini,
and tomatoes cooked in a low-fat "custard" with a cheese crust.

Serves 4

CALORIES PER SERVING: 319 • FAT CONTENT PER SERVING: 10.3 G

INGREDIENTS

12 ounces lean ground beef
1 large onion, finely chopped
1 tsp dried mixed herbs
1 tbsp all-purpose flour
1¼ cups beef stock
1 tbsp tomato paste
2 large tomatoes, thinly sliced
4 medium zucchini, thinly sliced

2 tbsp cornstarch
1¼ cups skim milk
⅔ cup low-fat unsweetened yogurt
1 medium egg yolk
4 tbsp Parmesan cheese,
freshly grated
salt and pepper

TO SERVE:
crusty bread
steamed vegetables

1 Preheat the oven to 375°F. In a large pan, dry-fry the beef and onion for 4–5 minutes until browned.

2 Stir in the herbs, flour, stock, and tomato paste, and season. Bring to a boil and simmer for 30 minutes until thickened.

3 Transfer the beef mixture to an ovenproof gratin dish.

Cover with a layer of the sliced tomatoes and then add a layer of sliced zucchini. Set aside until it is required.

4 Blend the cornstarch with a little milk in a small bowl. Pour the remaining milk into a saucepan and bring to a boil. Add the cornstarch mixture and cook, stirring, for 1–2 minutes, until thickened. Remove from the heat

and beat in the yogurt and egg yolk. Season with salt and pepper to taste.

5 Spread the white sauce over the layer of zucchini. Place the dish on a cookie sheet and sprinkle with grated Parmesan. Bake in the oven for 25–30 minutes, until golden brown. Serve with lots of fresh crusty bread and steamed vegetables.

Sweet & Sour Venison Stir-fry

*Venison is super-lean and low in fat, so it's the perfect choice for
a low-fat diet. Cooked quickly with crisp vegetables, it's ideal in a stir-fry.*

Serves 4

CALORIES PER SERVING: 174 • FAT CONTENT PER SERVING: 1.9 G

INGREDIENTS

1 bunch scallions
1 red bell pepper
3 1/2 ounces snow peas
3 1/2 ounces baby corn cobs
12 ounces lean venison steak
1 tbsp vegetable oil

1 clove garlic, crushed
1-inch piece fresh ginger root,
 finely chopped
3 tbsp light soy sauce, plus extra
 for serving
1 tbsp white wine vinegar

2 tbsp dry sherry
2 tsp clear honey
8 ounce can pineapple pieces in
 natural juice, drained
1 ounce bean sprouts
freshly cooked rice, to serve

1 Trim the scallions and cut into 1-inch pieces. Halve and seed the bell pepper and cut it into 1-inch pieces. Top and tail the snow peas and trim the baby corn cobs.

2 Trim the excess fat from the meat and cut it into thin strips. Heat the oil in a large skillet or preheated wok until hot and stir-fry the meat, garlic, and ginger for 5 minutes.

3 Add the prepared scallion, bell pepper, snow peas, and baby corn cobs to the pan, then add the soy sauce, vinegar, sherry, and honey. Stir-fry for a further 5 minutes, keeping the heat high.

4 Carefully stir in the pineapple pieces and bean sprouts and cook for a further 1–2 minutes to heat through. Serve with freshly cooked rice and extra soy sauce for dipping.

VARIATION

For a quick and nutritious meal-in-one, cook 8 ounces egg noodles in boiling water for 3–4 minutes. Drain well and add to the pan in step 4, together with the pineapple and bean sprouts. Stir well to mix. You will have to add an extra 2 tbsp soy sauce with the pineapple and bean sprouts so that the stir-fry does not dry out.

Venison & Garlic Mash

*Rich game is best served with a sweet fruit sauce. These small, tender
steaks of venison are cooked with sweet, juicy prunes and redcurrant jelly.*

Serves 4

CALORIES PER SERVING: 503 • FAT CONTENT PER SERVING: 6.1 G

INGREDIENTS

8 medallions of venison,
  2³/₄ ounces each
1 tbsp vegetable oil
1 red onion, chopped
²/₃ cup fresh beef stock
²/₃ cup red wine
3 tbsp redcurrant jelly

3¹/₂ ounces dried, pitted prunes
2 tsp cornstarch
2 tbsp brandy
salt and pepper

GARLIC MASH:
2 pounds potatoes, peeled and diced
¹/₂ tsp garlic paste
2 tbsp low-fat unsweetened yogurt
4 tbsp fresh parsley, chopped

1 Trim off any excess fat from the meat and season with salt and pepper on both sides.

2 Heat the oil in a skillet and fry the medallions with the onions on a high heat for 2 minutes on each side until browned all over.

3 Lower the heat and pour in the stock and wine. Add the redcurrant jelly and prunes and stir until the jelly melts. Bring to a boil, cover, and simmer for 10 minutes until cooked through.

4 Meanwhile, make the garlic mash. Place the potatoes in a saucepan and add enough water to cover. Bring to a boil and cook for 8–10 minutes, until tender. Drain well.

5 Mash the potatoes. Add the garlic paste, yogurt, and parsley and blend thoroughly. Season, set aside, and keep warm.

6 Remove the medallions from the skillet with a slotted spoon and keep warm.

7 Blend the cornstarch with the brandy in a small bowl and add to the pan juices. Heat, stirring, until thickened. Season with salt and pepper to taste.

8 Transfer the venison to serving plates and serve with the redcurrant and prune sauce and garlic mash.

Venison Meatballs with Sherried Kumquat Sauce

The sharp, citrusy flavor of kumquats is the perfect complement to these tasty steamed meatballs. Serve simply on a bed of pasta or noodles with some fresh vegetables.

Serves 4

CALORIES PER SERVING: 178 • FAT CONTENT PER SERVING: 2.1 G

INGREDIENTS

1 pound lean ground venison
1 small leek, finely chopped
1 medium carrot, finely grated
$\frac{1}{2}$ tsp ground nutmeg
1 medium egg white, lightly beaten
salt and pepper

TO SERVE:
freshly cooked pasta or noodles
freshly cooked vegetables

SAUCE:
$3\frac{1}{2}$ ounces kumquats

$\frac{1}{2}$ ounce superfine sugar
$\frac{2}{3}$ cup water
4 tbsp dry sherry
1 tsp cornstarch

1 Place the venison in a mixing bowl, together with the leek, carrot, seasoning, and nutmeg. Add the egg white and bind the ingredients together with your hands until the mixture is well molded and firm.

2 Divide the mixture into 16 equal portions. Using your fingers, form each portion into a small, round ball.

3 Bring a large saucepan of water to a boil. Arrange the meatballs on a layer of baking parchment in a steamer or large strainer and place over the boiling water. Cover and steam for 10 minutes, until cooked through.

4 Meanwhile, make the sauce. Wash and thinly slice the kumquats. Place them in a saucepan with the sugar and water and bring to a boil. Simmer for 2–3 minutes until tender.

5 Blend the sherry and cornstarch together and add to the pan. Heat through, stirring, until the sauce thickens. Season.

6 Drain the meatballs and transfer to a serving plate. Spoon the sauce on top and serve with pasta and vegetables.

Fruity Lamb Casserole

The sweet spicy blend of cinnamon, coriander, and cumin is the perfect foil for the tender lamb and apricots in this warming casserole

Serves 4

CALORIES PER SERVING: 280 • FAT CONTENT PER SERVING: 11.6 G

INGREDIENTS

1 pound lean lamb, trimmed and cut into 1-inch cubes
1 tsp ground cinnamon
1 tsp ground coriander
1 tsp ground cumin
2 tsp olive oil
1 medium red onion, finely chopped

1 garlic clove, crushed
14 ounce can chopped tomatoes
2 tbsp tomato paste
4$\frac{1}{2}$ ounces dried apricots
1 tsp superfine sugar
1$\frac{1}{4}$ cups vegetable stock
salt and pepper

1 small bunch fresh cilantro, to garnish
brown rice, steamed couscous, or bulgar wheat, to serve

1 Preheat the oven to 350°F. Place the meat in a mixing bowl and add the cinnamon, coriander, cumin, and oil. Mix thoroughly so that the lamb is coated in the spices.

2 Heat a nonstick skillet for a few seconds until it is hot, then add the spiced lamb. Reduce the heat and cook for 4–5 minutes, stirring, until browned all over. Using a slotted spoon, remove the lamb and transfer to a large casserole.

3 In the same skillet, cook the onion, garlic, tomatoes, and tomato paste for 5 minutes. Season to taste. Stir in the apricots and sugar, add the stock, and bring to a boil.

4 Spoon the sauce over the lamb and mix well. Cover and cook in the oven for 1 hour, removing the lid for the last 10 minutes.

5 Roughly chop the cilantro and sprinkle over the casserole to garnish. Serve with boiled brown rice, steamed couscous, or bulgar wheat.

Lamb, Bell Pepper, & Couscous

Couscous is a dish that originated among the Berbers, and it is a staple of North Africa. When it is steamed, it is a delicious plump grain, ideal for serving with a stew.

Serves 4

CALORIES PER SERVING: 522 • FAT CONTENT PER SERVING: 12.5 G

INGREDIENTS

2 medium red onions, sliced

juice of 1 lemon

1 large red bell pepper, seeded and thickly sliced

1 large green bell pepper, seeded and thickly sliced

1 large orange bell pepper, seeded and thickly sliced

pinch of saffron strands

cinnamon stick, broken

1 tbsp clear honey

1 1/4 cups vegetable stock

2 tsp olive oil

12 ounces lean lamb fillet, trimmed and sliced

1 tsp harissa paste

7 ounce can chopped tomatoes

15 ounce can garbanzo beans, drained

12 ounces couscous

2 tsp ground cinnamon

salt and pepper

1 Toss the onions in the lemon juice and transfer to a saucepan. Mix in the bell peppers, saffron, cinnamon stick, and honey. Pour in the stock, bring to a boil, cover, and simmer for 5 minutes.

2 Meanwhile, heat the oil in a skillet and gently fry the lamb for 3–4 minutes, until it is well browned all over.

3 Using a slotted spoon, drain the lamb and transfer it to the pan with the onions and peppers. Season and stir in the harissa paste, tomatoes, and garbanzo beans. Mix well, bring back to a boil, and simmer, uncovered, for 20 minutes.

4 Meanwhile, soak the couscous, following the instructions on the packet. Bring a saucepan of water to a boil. Transfer the couscous to a steamer or strainer lined with cheesecloth and place over the pan of boiling water. Cover and steam as directed.

5 Transfer the couscous to a warm serving platter and dust with ground cinnamon. Discard the cinnamon stick and spoon the stew over the couscous to serve.

Hot Pot Chops

A hot pot is a lamb casserole, made with carrots and onions and with a potato topping, that is traditionally made in the North of England. The chops used here are an interesting alternative.

Serves 4

CALORIES PER SERVING: 252 • FAT CONTENT PER SERVING: 11.3 G

INGREDIENTS

4 lean, boned lamb leg steaks, about 4½ ounces each

1 small onion, thinly sliced

1 medium carrot, thinly sliced

1 medium potato, thinly sliced

1 tsp olive oil

1 tsp dried rosemary

salt and pepper

fresh rosemary, to garnish

freshly steamed green vegetables, to serve

1 Preheat the oven to 350°F. Using a sharp knife, trim any excess fat from the lamb steaks.

2 Season both sides of the steaks well with salt and pepper and arrange them on a cookie sheet or ovenproof dish.

3 Alternate layers of sliced onion, carrot, and potato on top of each lamb steak.

4 Brush the tops of the potato lightly with oil, season well with salt and pepper to taste, and then sprinkle with a little dried rosemary.

5 Bake the hot pot chops in the oven for about 25–30 minutes, until the lamb is tender and cooked through.

6 Drain the lamb on absorbent paper towels and transfer to a warmed serving plate. Garnish with fresh rosemary and serve accompanied with a selection of green vegetables.

VARIATION

This recipe would work equally well with boneless chicken breasts. Pound the chicken slightly with a meat mallet or covered rolling pin so that the pieces are the same thickness throughout.

Minty Lamb Burgers

A tasty alternative to traditional hamburgers, these lamb burgers are flavored with mint and are accompanied with a smooth minty dressing.

Serves 4

CALORIES PER SERVING: 237 • FAT CONTENT PER SERVING: 7.8 G

INGREDIENTS

12 ounces lean lamb, ground
1 medium onion, finely chopped
4 tbsp dry whole-wheat breadcrumbs
2 tbsp mint jelly
salt and pepper

TO SERVE:
4 whole-wheat rolls, split
2 large tomatoes, sliced
small piece of cucumber, sliced
lettuce leaves

RELISH:
4 tbsp low-fat unsweetened yogurt
1 tbsp mint jelly, softened
2-inch piece of cucumber, finely diced
1 tbsp fresh mint, chopped

1 Place the lamb in a large bowl and mix in the onion, breadcrumbs, and jelly. Season well, then mold the ingredients together with your hands to form a firm mixture.

2 Divide the mixture into 4 and shape each portion into a round measuring 4 inches across. Place the rounds on a plate lined with baking parchment and leave to chill for 30 minutes.

3 Preheat the broiler. Line a broiler rack with baking parchment, securing the ends under the rack, and place the burgers on top. Cook for 8 minutes, then turn over the burgers, and cook for a further 7 minutes, or until completely cooked through.

4 Meanwhile, make the relish. Mix together the unsweetened yogurt, mint jelly, cucumber, and freshly chopped mint in a bowl. Cover and chill in the refrigerator until it is required.

5 Drain the burgers on absorbent paper towels. Serve the burgers inside the rolls and top with sliced tomatoes, cucumber, lettuce, and relish.

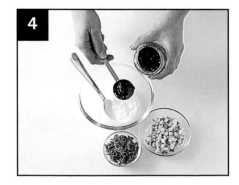

Tricolor Chicken & Spinach Lasagne

A delicious pasta bake that is filled with the colors of the Italian flag—red from the tomatoes, green from the spinach and pasta, and white from the chicken and the sauce.

Serves 4

CALORIES PER SERVING: 424 • FAT CONTENT PER SERVING: 7.2 G

INGREDIENTS

12 ounces frozen chopped spinach, thawed and drained

1/2 tsp ground nutmeg

1 pound lean, cooked chicken, skinned and diced

4 sheets precooked lasagne verde

1 1/2 tbsp cornstarch

1 3/4 cups skim milk

4 tbsp Parmesan cheese, freshly grated

salt and pepper

freshly prepared salad, to serve

TOMATO SAUCE:

14 ounce can chopped tomatoes

1 medium onion, finely chopped

1 garlic clove, crushed

2/3 cup white wine

3 tbsp tomato paste

1 tsp dried oregano

1 Preheat the oven to 400°F. To make the tomato sauce, place the tomatoes in a saucepan and stir in the onion, garlic, wine, tomato paste, and oregano. Bring to a boil and simmer for 20 minutes, until thick. Season well with salt and pepper.

2 Drain the spinach again and spread it out on absorbent paper towels to make sure that as much water as possible has been removed. Layer the spinach in the base of an ovenproof baking dish. Sprinkle with nutmeg and season.

3 Arrange the diced chicken over the spinach, and spoon the tomato sauce on top. Arrange the sheets of lasagne over the tomato sauce.

4 Blend the cornstarch with a little of the milk to make a paste. Pour the remaining milk into a saucepan and stir in the cornstarch paste. Heat for 2–3 minutes, stirring, until the sauce thickens. Season with salt and pepper to taste.

5 Spoon the sauce over the lasagne and transfer the dish to a cookie sheet. Sprinkle the grated cheese over the sauce and bake in the oven for 25 minutes, until golden-brown. Serve with a fresh green salad.

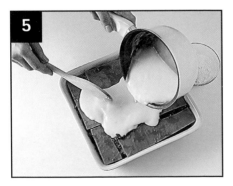

Chicken Pasta Bake with Fennel & Raisins

Tender lean chicken is baked with pasta quills in a creamy, low-fat cheese sauce with a hint of aniseed and the sweetness of juicy raisins.

Serves 4

CALORIES PER SERVING: 521 • FAT CONTENT PER SERVING: 15.5 G

INGREDIENTS

2 bulbs fennel

2 medium red onions, finely shredded

1 tbsp lemon juice

4^1/$_2$ ounces button mushrooms

1 tbsp olive oil

8 ounces penne (pasta quills)

^{1}/$_3$ cup raisins

8 ounces lean, boneless cooked chicken, skinned and shredded

13 ounces low-fat soft cheese with garlic and herbs

4^1/$_2$ ounces low-fat mozzarella cheese, thinly sliced

2 tbsp Parmesan cheese, grated

salt and pepper

1 Preheat the oven to 400°F. Trim the fennel and reserve the green fronds for garnishing the finished dish. Slice the fennel bulbs thinly. Generously coat the onion in the lemon juice. Quarter the mushrooms.

2 Heat the oil in a large skillet and sauté the fennel, onion, and mushrooms for 4–5 minutes, stirring, until just softened. Season well, transfer the vegetable mixture to a large mixing bowl, and set aside.

3 Bring a pan of lightly salted water to a boil and cook the penne according to the instructions on the packet until *al dente* (just cooked). Drain and mix the pasta with the vegetables.

4 Stir the raisins and chicken into the pasta mixture. Soften the soft cheese by beating it, then mix into the pasta and chicken— the heat from the pasta should make the cheese melt slightly.

5 Put the mixture into an ovenproof baking dish and transfer to a cookie sheet. Arrange slices of mozzarella cheese over the top and sprinkle with the grated Parmesan. Bake in the oven for 20–25 minutes, until golden-brown. Garnish with chopped fennel fronds and serve hot.

Baked Southern-style Chicken

Traditionally, this dish is deep-fried, but the low-fat version is just as mouthwatering. Serve with chunky potato wedges for a really authentic meal.

Serves 4

CALORIES PER SERVING: 402 • FAT CONTENT PER SERVING: 7.4 G

INGREDIENTS

4 baking potatoes, 8 ounces each
1 tbsp sunflower oil
2 tsp coarse sea salt
2 tbsp all-purpose flour
pinch of cayenne pepper

$^1/_2$ tsp paprika
$^1/_2$ tsp dried thyme
8 chicken drumsticks, skin removed
1 medium egg, beaten
2 tbsp cold water

6 tbsp dry white breadcrumbs
salt and pepper

TO SERVE:
low-fat coleslaw salad
corn relish

1 Preheat the oven to 400°F. Wash and scrub the potatoes and cut each into 8 equal portions. Place in a clean plastic bag and add the oil. Seal and shake the bag well to coat.

2 Arrange the potato wedges, skin side down, on a nonstick cookie sheet, sprinkle with the sea salt, and bake in the oven for 30–35 minutes, until they are tender and golden.

3 Meanwhile, mix the flour, spices, thyme, and seasoning together on a plate. Press the chicken drumsticks into the seasoned flour to lightly coat.

4 On one plate mix together the egg and water. On another plate sprinkle the breadcrumbs. Dip the chicken drumsticks first in the egg, and then in the breadcrumbs. Place on a nonstick cookie sheet.

5 Bake the chicken drumsticks alongside the potato wedges for 30 minutes, turning after 15 minutes, until they are tender and cooked through.

6 Drain the potato wedges thoroughly on absorbent paper towels to remove any excess fat, and serve with the chicken, accompanied with low-fat coleslaw and corn relish, if desired.

Lime Chicken Skewers with Mango Salsa

These succulent chicken kabobs are coated in a sweet lime dressing and are best served with a lime and mango relish. They make a refreshing light meal.

Serves 4

CALORIES PER SERVING: 200 • FAT CONTENT PER SERVING: 1.5 G

INGREDIENTS

4 boneless, skinless chicken breasts, about $4^1/2$ ounces each
3 tbsp lime marmalade
1 tsp white wine vinegar
$^1/_2$ tsp lime rind, finely grated
1 tbsp lime juice

salt and pepper

TO SERVE:
lime wedges
boiled white rice, sprinkled with chili powder

SALSA:
1 small mango
1 small red onion
1 tbsp lime juice
1 tbsp chopped fresh cilantro

1 Slice the chicken breasts into thin pieces and thread onto 8 skewers so that the meat forms an S-shape down each skewer.

2 Preheat the broiler. Arrange the chicken skewers on the broiler rack. Mix together the marmalade, vinegar, lime rind, and juice. Season with salt and pepper to taste. Brush the dressing generously over the chicken and

broil for 5 minutes. Turn the chicken over, brush with the dressing again, and broil for a further 4-5 minutes, until the chicken is cooked through.

3 Meanwhile, prepare the salsa. Peel the mango and slice the flesh off the smooth, central pit, using a sharp knife. Dice the flesh into small pieces and place in a small bowl.

4 Peel and finely chop the onion and mix into the mango, together with the lime juice and chopped cilantro. Season, cover, and chill until it is required.

5 Transfer the chicken kabobs to serving plates and serve with the salsa, accompanied with wedges of lime and boiled rice sprinkled with chili powder.

Sage Chicken & Rice

Cooking in a single pot means that all of the flavors are retained.
This is a substantial meal that needs only a salad and some crusty bread.

Serves 4

CALORIES PER SERVING: 391 • FAT CONTENT PER SERVING: 3.9 G

INGREDIENTS

1 large onion, chopped
1 garlic clove, crushed
2 celery stalks, sliced
2 carrots, diced
2 sprigs fresh sage
1¼ cups chicken stock
12 ounces boneless, skinless
   chicken breasts

1⅓ cups mixed brown and wild rice
14 ounce can chopped tomatoes
dash of Tabasco sauce
2 medium zucchini, trimmed and
   thinly sliced
3½ ounces lean ham, diced
salt and pepper
fresh sage, to garnish

TO SERVE:
salad greens
crusty bread

1 Place the onion, garlic, celery, carrots, and sprigs of fresh sage in a large saucepan and pour in the chicken stock. Bring to a boil, cover the pan, and simmer for 5 minutes.

2 Cut the chicken into 1-inch cubes and stir into the pan with the vegetables. Cover the pan and continue to cook for a further 5 minutes.

3 Stir in the rice and chopped tomatoes. Add a dash of Tabasco sauce to taste and season well. Bring to a boil, cover, and simmer for 25 minutes.

4 Stir in the sliced zucchini and diced ham and continue to cook, uncovered, for a further 10 minutes, stirring occasionally, until the rice is just tender.

5 Remove and discard the sprigs of sage. Garnish with a few sage leaves and serve with a fresh salad and crusty bread.

COOK'S TIP

If you do not have fresh sage, use 1 tsp of dried sage in step 1.

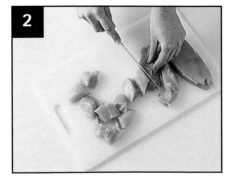

Chili Chicken & Corn Meatballs

Tender chicken nuggets are served with a sweet and sour sauce.

Serves 4

CALORIES PER SERVING: 223 • FAT CONTENT PER SERVING: 3 G

INGREDIENTS

1 pound lean ground chicken
4 scallions, trimmed and
  finely chopped
1 small red chili, seeded and finely
  chopped
1-inch piece fresh ginger root,
  finely chopped
3$^{1}/_{2}$ ounce can corn (no added sugar
  or salt), drained
salt and white pepper

TO SERVE:
boiled jasmine rice
chives, snipped

SAUCE:
$^{2}/_{3}$ cup fresh chicken stock
3$^{1}/_{2}$ ounces cubed pineapple in
  natural juice, drained, with
  4 tbsp reserved juice
1 medium carrot, cut into thin strips

1 small red bell pepper, seeded
  and diced
1 small green bell pepper, seeded
  and diced
1 tbsp light soy sauce
2 tbsp rice vinegar
1 tbsp superfine sugar
1 tbsp tomato paste
2 tsp cornstarch mixed to a paste
  with 4 tsp cold water

1 To make the meatballs, place the chicken in a bowl and add the scallions, chili, ginger, seasoning, and corn. Mix together with your hands.

2 Divide the mixture into 16 portions and form each into a ball. Bring a saucepan of water to a boil. Put the meatballs on a sheet of baking parchment in a steamer or large strainer, place over the water, cover, and steam for 10–12 minutes.

3 To make the sauce, pour the stock and pineapple juice into a saucepan and bring to a boil. Add the carrot and bell peppers, cover, and simmer for 5 minutes.

4 Stir in the remaining ingredients and heat through, stirring, until thickened. Season and set aside until required.

5 Drain the meatballs and transfer to a serving plate. Garnish with snipped chives and serve with boiled rice and the sauce (re-heated if necessary).

Crispy-Topped Stuffed Chicken

An attractive main course of chicken breasts filled with mixed bell peppers and set on a sea of red bell peppers and tomato sauce.

Serves 4

CALORIES PER SERVING: 211 • FAT CONTENT PER SERVING: 3.8 G

INGREDIENTS

4 boneless, skinless chicken breasts, about 5¹/₂ ounces each

4 sprigs fresh tarragon

¹/₂ small orange bell pepper, seeded and sliced

¹/₂ small green bell pepper, seeded and sliced

¹/₂ ounce whole-wheat breadcrumbs

1 tbsp sesame seeds

4 tbsp lemon juice

1 small red bell pepper, halved and seeded

7 ounce can chopped tomatoes

1 small red chili, seeded and chopped

¹/₄ tsp celery salt

salt and pepper

fresh tarragon, to garnish

1 Preheat the oven to 400°F. Slit the chicken breasts with a small, sharp knife to create a pocket in each. Season inside each pocket with salt and pepper to taste.

2 Place a sprig of tarragon and a few slices of orange and green bell peppers in each pocket. Place the chicken breasts on a nonstick cookie sheet and sprinkle with the breadcrumbs and sesame seeds.

3 Spoon 1 tbsp lemon juice over each chicken breast and bake in the oven for 35–40 minutes, until the chicken is tender and cooked through.

4 Meanwhile, preheat the broiler. Arrange the red bell pepper halves, skin side up, on the rack and cook for 5–6 minutes, until the skin blisters. Leave to cool for 10 minutes, then peel off the skins.

5 Put the red bell pepper in a blender, add the tomatoes, chili, and celery salt, and process for a few seconds. Season to taste. Alternatively, chop the red bell pepper and rub through a strainer with the tomatoes and chili.

6 When the chicken is cooked, heat the sauce, spoon a little onto a warm plate, and arrange a chicken breast in the center. Garnish with tarragon and serve.

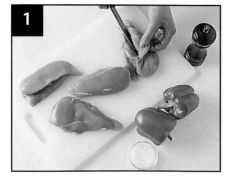

Chicken with a Curried Yogurt Crust

A spicy, Indian-style coating is baked around lean chicken to give a full flavor.
Serve hot or cold with a tomato, cucumber, and cilantro relish.

Serves 4

CALORIES PER SERVING: 176 • FAT CONTENT PER SERVING: 2 G

INGREDIENTS

1 garlic clove, crushed
1-inch piece fresh ginger root,
   finely chopped
1 fresh green chili, seeded and
   finely chopped
6 tbsp low-fat unsweetened yogurt
1 tbsp tomato paste
1 tsp ground turmeric

1 tsp garam masala
1 tbsp lime juice
4 boneless, skinless chicken breasts,
   each 4$\frac{1}{2}$ ounces
salt and pepper
wedges of lime or lemon, to serve

RELISH:
4 medium tomatoes
$\frac{1}{4}$ cucumber
1 small red onion
2 tbsp chopped fresh cilantro

1 Preheat the oven to 375°F. In a small bowl mix together the garlic, ginger, chili, yogurt, tomato paste, turmeric, garam masala, lime juice, and seasoning.

2 Wash and pat dry the chicken breasts with paper towels and place them on a cookie sheet. Brush or spread the spicy yogurt mix over the chicken and bake in the oven for 30–35 minutes until

the meat is tender and thoroughly cooked through.

3 Meanwhile, make the relish. Finely chop the tomatoes, cucumber, and onion and mix together with the cilantro. Season, cover, and chill until required.

4 Drain the cooked chicken on absorbent paper towels and serve hot with the relish.

Alternatively, allow to cool, chill for at least 1 hour, and serve sliced as part of a salad.

VARIATION

The spicy yogurt coating would work just as well if spread on a chunky white fish, such as cod fillet. The cooking time should be reduced to 15–20 minutes.

Broiled Chicken with Lemon & Honey

A good dish for the barbecue, this sweet and citrusy chicken can be served hot or cold. Sesame-flavored noodles are the ideal accompaniment for the hot version.

Serves 4

CALORIES PER SERVING: 403 • FAT CONTENT PER SERVING: 4.7 G

INGREDIENTS

4 boneless, skinless chicken breasts, about 4¹/₂ ounces each
2 tbsp clear honey
1 tbsp dark soy sauce
1 tsp finely grated lemon rind
1 tbsp lemon juice

salt and pepper

TO GARNISH:
1 tbsp fresh chives, chopped
lemon rind, finely grated

NOODLES:
8 ounces rice noodles
2 tsp sesame oil
1 tbsp sesame seeds
1 tsp finely grated lemon rind

1 Preheat the broiler. Trim the chicken breasts to remove any excess fat, then wash, and pat dry with absorbent paper towels. Using a sharp knife, score the chicken breasts with a criss-cross pattern on both sides (making sure that you do not cut all the way through the meat).

2 Carefully mix together the honey, soy sauce, lemon rind, and juice in a small bowl, and then season well with a little black pepper.

3 Arrange the chicken breasts on the broiler rack and brush with half the honey mixture. Cook for 10 minutes, turn over, and brush with the remaining mixture. Cook for a further 8–10 minutes, or until cooked through.

4 Meanwhile, prepare the noodles according to the instructions on the packet. Drain well and pile into a warm serving bowl. Mix the noodles with the sesame oil, sesame seeds, and the lemon rind. Season and keep warm.

5 Drain the chicken and serve with a small mound of noodles, garnished with chopped chives and lemon zest.

VARIATION

For a different flavor, replace the lemon with orange or lime. If you prefer, serve the chicken with boiled rice or pasta, which you can flavor with sesame seeds and citrus rind in the same way.

Chicken & Plum Casserole

Full of the flavors of fall, this combination of lean chicken, shallots, garlic, and fresh, juicy plums is a very fruity blend. Serve with bread to mop up the gravy.

Serves 4

CALORIES PER SERVING: 285 • FAT CONTENT PER SERVING: 6.4 G

INGREDIENTS

2 slices lean bacon, chopped
1 tbsp sunflower oil
1 pound skinned, boned chicken
   thighs, cut into 4 equal strips
1 garlic clove, crushed
6 ounces shallots, halved

8 ounces plums, halved or quartered
   (if large) and pitted
1 tbsp. light muscovado sugar
$^2/_3$ cup dry sherry
2 tbsp plum sauce
2 cups fresh chicken stock

2 tsp cornstarch mixed with 4 tsp
   cold water
2 tbsp chopped fresh parsley,
   to garnish
crusty bread, to serve

1 In a large, nonstick skillet, dry fry the bacon for 2–3 minutes, until the juices run out.

2 Remove the bacon from the pan with a slotted spoon, set aside, and keep warm.

3 In the same skillet, heat the oil and fry the chicken with the garlic and shallots for 4–5 minutes, stirring occasionally, until well browned all over.

4 Return the bacon to the skillet and stir in the plums, sugar, sherry, plum sauce, and stock. Bring to a boil and simmer for 20 minutes, until the plums have softened and the chicken is cooked through.

5 Add the cornstarch mixture to the skillet and cook, stirring occasionally, for a further 2–3 minutes, until the mixture has thickened.

6 Spoon the casserole onto warm serving plates and garnish with chopped parsley. Serve with chunks of bread to mop up the fruity gravy.

VARIATION

Chunks of lean turkey or pork would also go well with this combination of flavors. The cooking time will remain the same.

Orange Turkey with Rice & Green Vegetables

This is a good way to use up leftover rice. You could use fresh or canned sweet pink grapefruit for an interesting alternative.

Serves 4

CALORIES PER SERVING: 354 • FAT CONTENT PER SERVING: 5.5 G

INGREDIENTS

1 tbsp olive oil
1 medium onion, chopped
1 pound skinless lean turkey (such as fillet), cut into thin strips
1¼ cups unsweetened orange juice
1 bay leaf

8 ounces small broccoli flowerets
1 large zucchini, diced
1 large orange
6 cups cooked brown rice
salt and pepper
tomato and onion salad, to serve

TO GARNISH:
1 ounce pitted black olives in brine, drained and quartered
bunch fresh basil leaves, shredded

1 Heat the oil in a large skillet and fry the onion and turkey, stirring, for 4–5 minutes, until lightly browned.

2 Pour in the orange juice and add the bay leaf and seasoning. Bring to a boil and simmer for 10 minutes.

3 Meanwhile, bring a large saucepan of water to a boil

and cook the broccoli flowerets, covered, for 2 minutes. Add the diced zucchini, bring back to a boil, cover, and cook for a further 3 minutes (do not overcook). Drain and set aside.

4 Using a sharp knife, peel off the skin and white pith from the orange. Slice down the orange to make thin, round slices, then cut each slice in half.

5 Stir the broccoli, zucchini, rice, and orange slices into the turkey mixture. Gently mix together and heat through for a further 3–4 minutes, until piping hot.

6 Transfer the turkey rice to warm serving plates and garnish with black olives and shredded basil leaves. Serve with a fresh tomato and onion salad.

Curried Turkey with Apricots & Golden Raisins

An easy-to-prepare supper dish of lean turkey in a fruit curry sauce served on a bed of spicy rice.

Serves 4

CALORIES PER SERVING: 418 • FAT CONTENT PER SERVING: 7.9 G

INGREDIENTS

1 tbsp vegetable oil
1 large onion, chopped
1 pound skinless turkey breast, cut into 1 inch cubes
3 tbsp mild curry paste
1$^1/_4$ cups fresh chicken stock
6 ounces frozen peas

14$^1/_2$ ounce can apricot halves in natural juice
$^1/_3$ cup golden raisins
6 cups Basmati rice, freshly cooked
1 tsp ground coriander
4 tbsp fresh cilantro, chopped

1 green chili, seeded and sliced
salt and pepper

1 Heat the oil in a large saucepan and gently fry the onion and turkey for 4–5 minutes, until the onion has softened and the turkey is a light golden color.

2 Stir in the curry paste. Pour in the stock, stirring, and bring to a boil. Cover and simmer for 15 minutes. Stir in the peas and bring back to a boil. Cover and simmer for 5 minutes.

3 Drain the apricots, reserving the juice, and cut into thick slices. Add to the curry, stirring in a little of the juice if the mixture is becoming dry. Add the golden raisins and cook for 2 minutes.

4 Mix the rice with the coriander and fresh cilantro, stir in the chili, and season well. Transfer the rice to warm plates and top with the curry.

VARIATION

Peaches can be used instead of the apricots if you prefer. Cook in exactly the same way.

Turkey Loaf with Zucchini & Tomato

An easy-to-make dish that looks impressive. Lean turkey, flavored with herbs and a layer of juicy tomatoes, is covered with zucchini ribbons.

Serves 6

CALORIES PER SERVING: 179 • FAT CONTENT PER SERVING: 2.7 G

INGREDIENTS

1 medium onion, finely chopped
1 garlic clove, crushed
2 pounds lean ground turkey
1 tbsp chopped fresh parsley

1 tbsp chopped fresh chives
1 tbsp chopped fresh tarragon
1 medium egg white, lightly beaten
1 medium and 1 large zucchini

2 medium tomatoes
salt and pepper
tomato and herb sauce, to serve

1 Preheat the oven to 375°F and line a nonstick loaf pan with baking parchment. Place the onion, garlic, and turkey in a bowl, add the herbs, and season well. Mix together with your hands, then add the egg white to bind.

2 Press half of the turkey mixture into the base of the pan. Thinly slice the medium zucchini and the tomatoes and arrange the slices over the meat.

Top with the rest of the turkey and press down firmly.

3 Cover with a layer of foil and place in a roasting pan. Pour in enough boiling water to come halfway up the sides of the pan. Bake in the oven for 1–1¼ hours, removing the foil for the last 20 minutes of cooking. Test the loaf by inserting a skewer into the center—the juices should run clear. The loaf will also shrink away from the sides of the pan.

4 Meanwhile, trim the large zucchini. Using a vegetable peeler or hand-held metal cheese slicer, cut the zucchini into thin ribbons. Bring a saucepan of water to a boil and blanch the zucchini ribbons for 1–2 minutes, until just tender. Drain thoroughly, set aside and keep warm.

5 Transfer the turkey loaf to a warm platter. Drape the zucchini ribbons over the loaf and serve with a tomato and herb sauce.

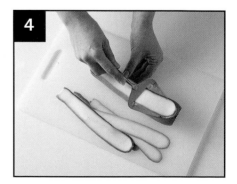

Duck with Kiwi Fruit & Raspberries

Duck is a rich meat and is best accompanied with fruit, as in this sophisticated dinner dish.

Serves 4

CALORIES PER SERVING: 286 • FAT CONTENT PER SERVING: 8.4 G

INGREDIENTS

1 pound boneless, skinless duck
   breasts
2 tbsp raspberry vinegar
2 tbsp brandy
1 tbsp clear honey
1 tsp sunflower oil

salt and pepper

TO SERVE:
2 kiwi fruit, peeled and sliced thinly
assorted vegetables

SAUCE:
8 ounces raspberries, thawed
   if frozen
1$\frac{1}{4}$ cups rosé wine
2 tsp cornstarch blended with 4 tsp
   cold water

1 Trim the duck breasts to remove any excess fat. Using a sharp knife, score the flesh in diagonal lines and then pound it with a meat mallet or a covered rolling pin until it is about ¾ inch thick.

2 Place the duck breasts in a shallow dish. Mix together the vinegar, brandy, and honey in a small bowl and pour it over the duck. Cover and chill in the refrigerator for about 1 hour. Preheat the broiler.

3 Drain the duck, reserving the marinade, and place on the broiler rack. Season and brush with a little oil. Cook for 10 minutes, turn over, season and brush with oil again, and cook for a further 8–10 minutes, until the meat is cooked through.

4 Meanwhile, make the sauce. Reserving about 2 ounces raspberries, place the rest in a pan. Add the reserved marinade and the wine. Bring to a boil and simmer for 5 minutes, until slightly reduced.

5 Strain the sauce through a strainer, pressing the raspberries with the back of a spoon. Return the liquid to the saucepan and add the cornstarch paste. Heat through, stirring, until thickened. Add the reserved raspberries and season to taste.

6 Thinly slice the duck breast and arrange fanned out on warm serving plates, alternating with slices of kiwi fruit. Pour on the sauce and serve with a selection of vegetables.

Roast Duck with Apples & Apricots

*If you cannot buy portions of duckling, use a whole bird and
cut it into joints. Always remove the skin before serving.*

Serves 4

CALORIES PER SERVING: 313 • FAT CONTENT PER SERVING: 6.5 G

INGREDIENTS

4 duckling portions, 12 ounces each
4 tbsp dark soy sauce
2 tbsp light muscovado sugar
2 red-skinned apples
2 green-skinned apples
juice of 1 lemon

2 tbsp clear honey
few bay leaves
salt and pepper
assorted fresh vegetables, to serve

SAUCE:
14^{1}/$_{2}$ ounce can apricots, in
    natural juice
4 tbsp sweet sherry

1 Preheat the oven to 375°F. Wash the duck and trim away any excess fat. Place on a wire rack over a roasting pan and prick all over with a fork.

2 Brush the duck with the soy sauce. Sprinkle on the sugar and season with pepper. Cook in the oven, basting occasionally, for 50–60 minutes, until the meat is cooked through—the juices should run clear when a skewer is inserted into the thickest part of the meat.

3 Meanwhile, core the apples and cut each into 6 wedges. Place in a bowl and mix with the lemon juice and honey. Transfer to a small roasting pan, add a few bay leaves, and season. Cook alongside the duck, basting occasionally, for 20–25 minutes, until tender. Discard the bay leaves.

4 To make the sauce, place the apricots in a blender or food processor, together with the juice from the can and the sherry.

Process for a few seconds until smooth. Alternatively, mash the apricots with a fork until smooth and mix with the juice and sherry.

5 Just before serving, heat the apricot paste in a small pan. Remove the skin from the duck and pat the flesh with paper towels to absorb any fat.

6 Serve the duck with the apple wedges and the apricot sauce, and accompanied with vegetables.

Fish & Shellfish

Naturally low in fat, yet rich in minerals and proteins, white fish and shellfish will be regular and important ingredients in any low-fat diet. There are so many flavors and textures available that the possible combinations are endless.

White fish, such as monkfish, haddock, cod, and turbot, are widely available and easy to cook. Shellfish, too, are low in fat and rich in flavor, and they can be cooked in a variety of ways to produce mouthwatering, low-fat dishes. Some fishes—salmon, tuna, trout, and mackerel, for example—are oily and should be eaten in moderation. They are rich in the fat-soluble vitamins A and D, however, and it is also believed that the oil in these fish is beneficial in breaking down cholesterol in the bloodstream.

Use this versatile ingredient in recipes that will soon become standards in your repertoire, from comforting Shrimp and Tuna Pasta Bake and Fish Cakes with Piquant Tomato Sauce, to sophisticated Five-spice Salmon with Ginger Stir-fry and Skewered Oriental Shellfish.

Shrimp & Tuna Pasta Bake

This dish is ideal for a substantial supper. You can use whatever pasta you like, but the tricolor varieties will give the most colorful results.

Serves 4

CALORIES PER SERVING: 470 • FAT CONTENT PER SERVING: 8.5 G

INGREDIENTS

8 ounces tricolor pasta shapes
1 tbsp vegetable oil
1 bunch scallions, trimmed
 and chopped
6 ounces button mushrooms, sliced
14 ounce can tuna in brine, drained
 and flaked

6 ounces peeled shrimp, thawed
 if frozen
2 tbsp cornstarch
$1^3/4$ cups skim milk
4 medium tomatoes, sliced thinly
1 ounce fresh breadcrumbs

1 ounce reduced-fat cheddar
 cheese, grated
salt and pepper

TO SERVE:
whole-wheat bread
fresh salad

1 Preheat the oven to 375°F. Bring a large saucepan of water to a boil and cook the pasta according to the instructions on the packet, until it is tender but still firm to the bite. Drain thoroughly.

2 Meanwhile, heat the oil in a skillet and sauté all but a handful of the scallions and all of the mushrooms, stirring, for 4–5 minutes until softened.

3 Place the cooked pasta in a bowl and mix in the scallions and mushrooms, tuna, and shrimp. Set aside and keep warm until required.

4 Blend the cornstarch with a little milk to make a paste. Pour the remaining milk into a saucepan and stir in the paste. Heat, stirring, until the sauce begins to thicken. Season with salt and pepper to taste.

5 Pour the sauce over the pasta mixture and stir until well combined. Transfer to the base of an ovenproof gratin dish and place on a cookie sheet.

6 Arrange the tomato slices over the pasta and sprinkle with the breadcrumbs and cheese. Bake for 25–30 minutes until golden. Serve sprinkled with the reserved scallions and accompanied with bread and salad.

Fish Cakes with Piquant Tomato Sauce

*The combination of pink- and white-fleshed fish transforms
the humble fish cake into something a bit special.*

Serves 4

CALORIES PER SERVING: 320 • FAT CONTENT PER SERVING: 7.5 G

INGREDIENTS

1 pound potatoes, diced
8 ounces haddock fillet
8 ounces trout fillet
1 bay leaf
1³/₄ cups fresh fish stock
2 tbsp low-fat unsweetened yogurt
4 tbsp fresh snipped chives
2³/₄ ounces dry white breadcrumbs

1 tbsp sunflower oil
salt and pepper
fresh snipped chives, to garnish
lemon wedges, to serve

PIQUANT TOMATO SAUCE:
³/₄ cup sieved tomatoes
4 tbsp dry white wine
4 tbsp low-fat unsweetened yogurt
chili powder

1 Place the potatoes in a saucepan and cover with water. Bring to a boil and cook for 10 minutes, or until tender. Drain well and mash.

2 Meanwhile, place the fish in a pan with the bay leaf and stock. Bring to a boil and simmer for 7–8 minutes, until tender. Remove the fish with a slotted spoon and flake the flesh away from the skin.

3 Gently mix the cooked fish with the potato, unsweetened yogurt, chives, and seasoning. Cool, then cover, and chill for 1 hour.

4 Sprinkle the breadcrumbs on a plate. Divide the fish mixture into 8 and form each portion into a patty, about 3 inches in diameter. Press each fish cake into the breadcrumbs, coating it all over.

5 Brush a skillet with oil and fry the fish cakes for 6 minutes. Turn the fish cakes over and cook for a further 5–6 minutes, until golden. Drain on paper towels and keep warm.

6 To make the sauce, heat the sieved tomatoes and wine. Season, remove from the heat, and stir in the yogurt. Return to the heat, sprinkle with chili powder, and serve with the fish cakes.

Provençal-style Mussels

These delicious large mussels are served hot with a tasty tomato and vegetable sauce.
If you can't find New Zealand mussels, serve the sauce with steamed fresh mussels.

Serves 4

CALORIES PER SERVING: 185 • FAT CONTENT PER SERVING: 6.5 G

INGREDIENTS

1 tbsp olive oil
1 large onion, finely chopped
1 garlic clove, finely chopped
1 small red bell pepper, seeded and
  finely chopped
sprig of rosemary
2 bay leaves
14 ounce can chopped tomatoes

$^2/_3$ cup white wine
1 zucchini, diced finely
2 tbsp tomato paste
1 tsp superfine sugar
$1^3/_4$ ounces pitted black olives in
  brine, drained, and chopped
$1^1/_2$ pounds cooked New Zealand
  mussels in their shells

1 tsp orange rind
salt and pepper
crusty bread, to serve

TO GARNISH:
2 tbsp chopped, fresh parsley
orange slices

1 Heat the oil in a large saucepan and gently sauté the onion, garlic, and bell pepper for 3–4 minutes, until just softened.

2 Add the sprig of rosemary and the bay leaves to the saucepan with the tomatoes and $^1/_3$ cup wine. Season with salt and pepper to taste, then bring to a boil, and simmer for about 15 minutes.

3 Stir in the zucchini, tomato paste, sugar, and olives. Simmer for 10 minutes.

4 Meanwhile, bring a pan of water to a boil. Arrange the mussels in a steamer or a large strainer and place over the water. Sprinkle with the remaining wine and the orange rind. Cover and steam until the mussels open (discard any that remain closed).

5 Remove the mussels with a slotted spoon and arrange on a warm serving plate. Discard the herbs and spoon the sauce over the mussels. Garnish with chopped parsley and orange slices, and serve.

COOK'S TIP

Chop the vegetables for the sauce as finely as possible for best results.

Fish & Rice with Dark Rum

Based on a traditional Cuban recipe, this dish is similar to Spanish paella, but it has the added kick of dark rum. A meal in one, it needs only a simple salad accompaniment.

Serves 4

CALORIES PER SERVING: 575 ● FAT CONTENT PER SERVING: 4.5 G

INGREDIENTS

1 pound firm white fish fillets (such as cod or monkfish), skinned and cut into 1-inch cubes
2 tsp ground cumin
2 tsp dried oregano
2 tbsp lime juice
²/₃ cup dark rum
1 tbsp dark muscovado sugar

3 garlic cloves, finely chopped
1 large onion, chopped
1 medium red bell pepper, seeded and sliced into rings
1 medium green bell pepper, seeded and sliced into rings
1 medium yellow bell pepper, seeded and sliced into rings

5 cups fish stock
2 cups long-grain rice
salt and pepper
crusty bread, to serve

TO GARNISH:
fresh oregano leaves
lime wedges

1 Place the cubes of fish in a bowl and add the cumin, oregano, salt, pepper, lime juice, rum, and sugar. Mix well, cover the bowl, and chill for about 2 hours.

2 Meanwhile, place the garlic, onion, and bell peppers in a large saucepan. Pour in the stock and stir in the rice. Bring to a boil, cover, and cook for 15 minutes.

3 Gently add the fish and the marinade juices to the pan. Bring back to a boil and simmer, uncovered, stirring occasionally but taking care not to break up the fish, for 10 minutes, until the fish is cooked and the rice is tender.

4 Season and transfer to a warm serving plate. Garnish with fresh oregano and lime wedges, and serve with crusty bread.

VARIATION

If you prefer, use unsweetened orange juice in the marinade instead of the rum.

Seafood Stir-fry

This combination of assorted seafood and tender vegetables delicately flavored with ginger makes an ideal light meal served with thread noodles.

Serves 4

CALORIES PER SERVING: 205 • FAT CONTENT PER SERVING: 6.5 G

INGREDIENTS

3¹/₂ ounces small, thin asparagus spears, trimmed

1 tbsp sunflower oil

1-inch piece fresh ginger root, cut into thin strips

1 medium leek, shredded

2 medium carrots, julienned

3¹/₂ ounces baby corn, quartered lengthwise

2 tbsp light soy sauce

1 tbsp oyster sauce

1 tsp clear honey

1 pound cooked, assorted shellfish, thawed if frozen

freshly cooked egg noodles, to serve

TO GARNISH:
4 large cooked shrimp
small bunch fresh chives

1 Bring a small saucepan of water to a boil and blanch the asparagus for 1–2 minutes. Drain the asparagus, set aside, and keep warm.

2 Heat the oil in a wok or large skillet and stir-fry the ginger, leek, carrot, and corn for about 3 minutes.

3 Add the soy sauce, oyster sauce, and honey to the wok or skillet. Stir in the shellfish and continue to stir-fry for 2–3 minutes until the vegetables are just tender and the shellfish is thoroughly heated through. Add the blanched asparagus to the wok or skillet and stir-fry for about 2 minutes.

4 To serve, pile the cooked noodles onto 4 warm serving plates and spoon the seafood and vegetable stir-fry on top. Serve garnished with a large shrimp and freshly snipped chives.

COOK'S TIP

When you are preparing dense vegetables, such as carrots and other root vegetables, for stir-frying, slice them into thin, evenly sized pieces so that they cook quickly and at the same rate. Delicate vegetables, such as bell peppers, leeks, and scallions, do not need to be cut as thinly.

Smoky Fish Pie

This flavorsome fish pie is perfect for a light supper.

Serves 4

CALORIES PER SERVING: 510 • FAT CONTENT PER SERVING: 6 G

INGREDIENTS

2 pounds smoked haddock or
  cod fillets
2¹/₂ cups skim milk
2 bay leaves
4 ounces button mushrooms,
  quartered
4 ounces frozen peas

4 ounces frozen corn kernels
1¹/₂ pounds potatoes, diced
5 tbsp low-fat unsweetened yogurt
4 tbsp chopped fresh parsley

2 ounces smoked salmon, sliced into
  thin strips
3 tbsp cornstarch
1 ounce smoked cheese, grated
salt and pepper
wedges of lemon, to garnish

1 Preheat the oven to 400°F. Place the fish in a pan and add the milk and bay leaves. Bring to a boil, cover, and then simmer for 5 minutes.

2 Add the mushrooms, peas, and corn to the pan, bring back to a simmer, cover, and cook for 5–7 minutes. Let cool.

3 Place the potatoes in a saucepan, cover with water, boil, and cook for 8 minutes.

Drain well and mash with a fork or a potato masher. Stir in the yogurt, parsley, and seasoning. Set aside.

4 Using a slotted spoon, remove the fish from the pan. Flake the cooked fish away from the skin and place in an ovenproof gratin dish. Reserve the cooking liquid.

5 Drain the vegetables, reserving the cooking liquid, and gently stir into the fish, together with the salmon strips.

6 Blend a little cooking liquid into the cornstarch to make a paste. Transfer the rest of the liquid to a saucepan and add the paste. Heat through, stirring, until thickened. Discard the bay leaves and season to taste.

7 Pour the sauce over the fish and vegetables. Spoon the mashed potato on top, covering the fish, sprinkle with cheese, and bake for 25–30 minutes. Garnish with lemon wedges and serve.

Seafood Spaghetti

You can use whatever combination of shellfish you like in this recipe—it is poached in a savory stock and served with freshly cooked spaghetti.

Serves 4

CALORIES PER SERVING: 400 • FAT CONTENT PER SERVING: 7 G

INGREDIENTS

2 tsp olive oil
1 small red onion, finely chopped
1 tbsp lemon juice
1 garlic clove, crushed
2 celery stalks, finely chopped
$^2/_3$ cup fresh fish stock

$^2/_3$ cup dry white wine
small bunch fresh tarragon
1 pound fresh mussels, prepared
8 ounces fresh shrimp, peeled
    and deveined
8 ounces baby squid, cleaned,
    trimmed, and sliced into rings

8 small cooked crab claws, cracked
    and peeled
8 ounces spaghetti
salt and pepper
2 tbsp chopped fresh tarragon,
    to garnish

1 Heat the oil in a large saucepan and sauté the onion with the lemon juice, garlic, and celery for 3–4 minutes, until just softened.

2 Pour in the stock and wine. Bring to a boil and add the tarragon and mussels. Cover and simmer for 5 minutes. Add the shrimp, squid, and crab claws to the pan, mix together, and cook for 3–4 minutes, until the mussels have opened, the shrimp are pink,

and the squid is opaque. Discard any mussels that have not opened, and the tarragon.

3 Meanwhile, cook the spaghetti in a saucepan of boiling water according to the instructions on the packet. Drain well.

4 Add the spaghetti to the shellfish mixture and toss together. Season with salt and pepper to taste.

5 Transfer to warm serving plates and spoon the cooking juices on top. Serve garnished with freshly chopped tarragon.

COOK'S TIP

Crab claws contain lean crabmeat. Ask your fish store to crack the claws for you, leaving the pincers intact, because the shell is very tough.

Chili- & Crab-stuffed Red Snapper

This popular fish is pinkish-red in color and has moist, tender flesh.
For this recipe it is steamed, but it can also be baked or braised.

Serves 4

CALORIES PER SERVING: 120 • FAT CONTENT PER SERVING: 1 G

INGREDIENTS

4 red snappers, cleaned and scaled,
   about 6 ounces each
2 tbsp dry sherry
salt and pepper
wedges of lime, to garnish

STUFFING:
1 small red chili
1 garlic clove
1 scallion
$^1/_2$ tsp finely grated lime rind
1 tbsp lime juice

$3^1/_2$ ounces white crabmeat, flaked

TO SERVE:
stir-fried shredded vegetables,
   boiled white rice

1 Rinse the fish and pat dry on absorbent paper towels. Season inside and out and place in a shallow dish. Spoon the sherry over the fish and set aside.

2 Meanwhile, make the stuffing. Carefully halve, seed, and finely chop the chili. Place in a small bowl.

3 Peel and finely chop the garlic. Trim and finely chop the scallion. Add to the chili together with the grated lime rind, lime juice, and the flaked crabmeat. Season with salt and pepper to taste and combine. Press some of the stuffing into the cavity of each fish.

4 Bring a large saucepan of water to a boil. Arrange the fish in a steamer lined with baking parchment or in a large strainer and place over a boiling water. Cover and steam for 10 minutes. Turn the fish over and steam for a further 10 minutes, or until the fish is cooked.

5 Drain the fish and transfer to a serving plate. Garnish with wedges of lime and serve with stir-fried vegetables and white rice.

COOK'S TIP

Always wash your hands thoroughly after handling chilies, as they can irritate your skin and eyes.

Citrus Fish Skewers

You can use your favorite fish for this dish, as long as it is firm enough to thread onto a skewer. The tang of orange makes this a refreshing light meal.

Serves 4

CALORIES PER SERVING: 335 • FAT CONTENT PER SERVING: 14.5 G

INGREDIENTS

1 pound firm white fish fillets (such as cod or monkfish)	1 bunch fresh bay leaves	salt and pepper
1 pound thick salmon fillet	1 tsp finely grated lemon rind	
2 large oranges	3 tbsp lemon juice	TO SERVE:
1 pink grapefruit	2 tsp clear honey	crusty bread
	2 garlic cloves, crushed	mixed salad

1 Skin the white fish and the salmon, rinse, and pat dry on absorbent paper towels. Cut each fillet into 16 pieces.

2 Using a sharp knife, remove the skin and pith from the oranges and grapefruit. Cut out the segments of flesh, removing all remaining traces of the pith and dividing membrane.

3 Thread the pieces of fish alternately with the orange and grapefruit segments and the bay leaves onto 8 skewers. Place the skewers in a shallow dish.

4 Mix together the lemon rind and juice, the honey, and garlic. Pour over the fish skewers and season well. Cover and chill for 2 hours, turning occasionally.

5 Preheat the broiler. Remove the skewers from the marinade and place on the rack. Cook for 7–8 minutes, turning once, until completely cooked through.

6 Drain, transfer to serving plates, and serve with crusty bread and a fresh salad.

VARIATION

This dish makes an unusual starter. Try it with any firm fish—shark or swordfish, for example—or with tuna for a meatier texture.

Seafood Pizza

A change from the standard pizza toppings, this dish has piles of seafood baked with a red bell pepper and tomato sauce on a dill-flavored bread base.

Serves 4

CALORIES PER SERVING: 315 • FAT CONTENT PER SERVING: 7 G

INGREDIENTS

5 ounces standard pizza base mix

4 tbsp chopped fresh dill *or* 2 tbsp dried dill

fresh dill, to garnish

SAUCE:

1 large red bell pepper

14 ounce can chopped tomatoes with onion and herbs

3 tbsp tomato paste

salt and pepper

TOPPING:

12 ounces assorted cooked seafood, thawed if frozen

1 tbsp capers in brine, drained

1 ounce pitted black olives in brine, drained

1 ounce low-fat mozzarella cheese, grated

1 tbsp grated, fresh Parmesan cheese

1 Preheat the oven to 400°F. Place the pizza base mix in a bowl and stir in the dill. Make the dough according to the instructions on the packet.

2 Press the dough into a round measuring 10 inches across on a cookie sheet lined with baking parchment. Set aside to rise.

3 Preheat the broiler. To make the sauce, halve and seed the bell pepper and arrange on a broiler rack. Cook for 8–10 minutes, until softened and charred. Leave to cool slightly, peel off the skin, and chop the flesh.

4 Place the tomatoes and bell pepper in a saucepan. Bring to a boil and simmer for 10 minutes.

Gradually stir in the tomato paste and season with salt and pepper to taste.

5 Spread the sauce over the pizza base and top with the seafood. Sprinkle the capers and olives, top with the cheeses, and bake for 25–30 minutes. Garnish with sprigs of dill and serve hot.

Pan-seared Halibut with Red Onion Relish

Liven up firm steaks of white fish with a spicy, colorful relish. You can use white onions if you prefer, but red onions have a slightly sweeter flavor.

Serves 4

CALORIES PER SERVING: 250 • FAT CONTENT PER SERVING: 8 G

INGREDIENTS

1 tsp olive oil
4 halibut steaks, skinned,
　6 ounces each
$^1/_2$ tsp cornstarch mixed with 2 tsp
　cold water
salt and pepper

2 tbsp fresh chives, snipped,
　to garnish

RED ONION RELISH:
2 medium red onions
6 shallots

1 tbsp lemon juice
2 tsp olive oil
2 tbsp red wine vinegar
2 tsp superfine sugar
$^2/_3$ cup fresh fish stock

1 To make the relish, peel and thinly shred the onions and shallots. Place in a small bowl and toss in the lemon juice.

2 Heat 2 tsp oil in a pan and sauté the onions and shallots for 3–4 minutes, until just softened.

3 Add the vinegar and sugar and continue to cook for a further 2 minutes on a high heat. Pour in the stock and season well. Bring to a boil and simmer gently for a further 8–9 minutes, until the sauce has thickened and is slightly reduced.

4 Brush a nonstick, ridged skillet with oil and heat until hot. Press the steaks into the pan to seal, lower the heat, and cook for 4 minutes. Turn the fish over and cook for 4–5 minutes, until cooked through. Drain on paper towels and keep warm.

5 Stir the cornstarch paste into the onion sauce and heat through, stirring, until thickened. Season to taste.

6 Pile the relish on to 4 warm serving plates and place a halibut steak on top of each.

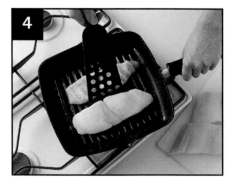

Five-spice Salmon with Ginger Stir-fry

Five-spice powder is a blend of star anise, fennel, cinnamon, cloves, and Szechwan peppercorns or fagara that is often used in Chinese dishes. It is a deliciously fragrant seasoning.

Serves 4

CALORIES PER SERVING: 295 • FAT CONTENT PER SERVING: 18 G

INGREDIENTS

4 salmon fillets, skinned,
    4 ounces each
2 tsp five-spice powder
pepper
1 large leek
1 large carrot

4 ounces snow peas
1-inch piece fresh ginger root
2 tbsp ginger wine
2 tbsp light soy sauce
1 tbsp vegetable oil
freshly boiled noodles, to serve

TO GARNISH:
leek, shredded
fresh ginger root, shredded
carrot, shredded

1 Wash the salmon and pat dry on absorbent paper towels. Rub the five-spice powder into both sides of the fish and season with freshly ground pepper. Set aside until required.

2 Using a sharp knife, trim the leek, slice it down the center, and rinse under cold water to remove any dirt. Finely shred the leek. Peel the carrot and cut it into very thin strips. Top and tail the snow peas and cut them into shreds. Peel the ginger and slice thinly into strips.

3 Place all of the vegetables into a large bowl and toss in the ginger wine and 1 tbsp soy sauce. Set aside.

4 Preheat the broiler. Place the salmon fillets on the rack and brush with the remaining soy sauce. Cook for 2–3 minutes on each side, until completely cooked through.

5 While the salmon is cooking, heat the oil in a nonstick wok or large skillet and stir-fry the vegetables for 5 minutes, until just tender. Take care that you do not overcook the vegetables—they should still have bite. Transfer to serving plates.

6 Drain the salmon on paper towels and serve on a bed of stir-fried vegetables. Garnish with shredded leek, ginger, and carrot and serve with noodles.

Skewered Oriental Shellfish

These shellfish and vegetable kabobs are ideal for serving at parties.
They are quick and easy to prepare and take next to no time to cook.

Makes 12

CALORIES PER SERVING: 100 • FAT CONTENT PER SERVING: 2.5 G

INGREDIENTS

12 ounces raw tiger shrimp, peeled
leaving tails intact
12 ounces scallops, cleaned,
trimmed, and halved
(quartered if large)
1 bunch scallions, sliced into
1-inch pieces
1 medium red bell pepper, seeded
and cubed

3$\frac{1}{2}$ ounces baby corn cobs, trimmed
and sliced into $\frac{1}{2}$-inch pieces
3 tbsp dark soy sauce
$\frac{1}{2}$ tsp hot chili powder
$\frac{1}{2}$ tsp ground ginger
1 tbsp sunflower oil
1 red chili, seeded and sliced

DIP:
4 tbsp dark soy sauce
4 tbsp dry sherry
2 tsp clear honey
1-inch piece fresh ginger root, peeled
and grated
1 scallion, trimmed and sliced
very finely

1 Soak 12 wooden skewers in cold water for 10 minutes to prevent them from burning.

2 Divide the shrimp, scallops, scallions, bell pepper, and baby corn into 12 portions and thread onto the skewers. Cover the ends with foil so that they do not burn, and place in a shallow dish.

3 Mix the soy sauce, chili powder, and ground ginger and coat the shellfish and vegetable kabobs. Cover and chill for about 2 hours.

4 Preheat the broiler. Arrange the skewers on the rack, brush the shellfish and vegetables with oil, and cook for 2–3 minutes on each side, until the shrimp turn

pink, the scallops become opaque, and the vegetables are soft.

5 Mix together the dip ingredients and set aside.

6 Remove the foil and transfer the kabobs to a warm serving platter. Garnish with sliced chili and serve with the dip.

Tuna Steaks with Fragrant Spices & Lime

Fresh tuna steaks are very meaty—they have a firm texture, yet the flesh is succulent. This recipe would be an impressive addition to a barbecue.

Serves 4

CALORIES PER SERVING: 200 • FAT CONTENT PER SERVING: 3.5 G

INGREDIENTS

4 tuna steaks, 6 ounces each
1/2 tsp finely grated lime rind
1 garlic clove, crushed
2 tsp olive oil
1 tsp ground cumin

1 tsp ground coriander
pepper
1 tbsp lime juice
2 tbsp chopped fresh cilantro

TO SERVE:
avocado relish (see Cook's Tip)
lime wedges

1 Trim the skin from the tuna steaks, rinse, and pat dry on absorbent paper towels.

2 In a small bowl, mix together the lime rind, garlic, olive oil, cumin, coriander, and pepper to make a paste.

3 Spread the paste thinly on both sides of the tuna. Heat a nonstick, ridged skillet until hot and press the tuna steaks into the pan to seal them. Lower the heat and cook for 5 minutes. Turn the fish over and cook for a further 4–5 minutes, until the fish is cooked through. Drain on absorbent paper towels and transfer to a serving plate.

4 Sprinkle the lime juice and chopped cilantro over the fish. Serve with freshly made avocado relish (see Cook's Tip) and lime wedges.

COOK'S TIP

For low-fat avocado relish to serve with tuna, peel and remove the pit from one small ripe avocado. Toss in 1 tbsp lime juice. Mix in 1 tbsp freshly chopped cilantro and 1 small finely chopped red onion. Stir in some chopped fresh mango or a chopped medium tomato and season well.

Baked Trout Mexican-style

You can make this dish as hot or as mild as you like by adding more or less red chili to suit your taste. The green chilies are milder and add a refreshing pungency to the dish.

Serves 4

CALORIES PER SERVING: 235 • FAT CONTENT PER RECIPE: 5.5 G

INGREDIENTS

4 trout, 8 ounces each
1 small bunch fresh cilantro
4 shallots, finely shredded
1 small yellow bell pepper, seeded
  and very finely chopped

1 small red bell pepper, seeded and
  very finely chopped
2 green chilies, seeded and
  finely chopped
1–2 red chilies, seeded and
  finely chopped

1 tbsp lemon juice
1 tbsp white wine vinegar
2 tsp superfine sugar
salt and pepper
fresh cilantro, to garnish

1 Preheat the oven to 350°F. Wash the trout and pat dry with absorbent paper towels. Season the cavities and fill them with a few cilantro leaves.

2 Place the fish side by side in a shallow ovenproof dish. Sprinkle on the shallots, bell peppers, and chilies.

3 Mix together the lemon juice, vinegar, and sugar in a bowl. Spoon over the trout and season with salt and pepper. Cover the dish and bake for 30 minutes, or until the fish is tender and the flesh is opaque.

4 Remove the fish with a fish slice and drain thoroughly. Transfer to warm serving plates and spoon the cooking juices over the fish. Garnish with fresh cilantro and serve immediately with chili bean rice, if you wish (see Cook's Tip).

COOK'S TIP

To make chili bean rice to serve with this recipe, cook 1¼ cups long-grain white rice in boiling water. Drain and return to the pan. Drain and rinse a 14 ounce can kidney beans and stir into the rice along with 1 tsp each of ground cumin and ground coriander. Stir in 4 tbsp freshly chopped cilantro and season well.

Vegetables & Salads

Too frequently, leaf vegetables are overcooked and limp, with all the goodness and flavor boiled out, while salads are often nothing more than a dismal leaf or two of pale green lettuce with a slice of tomato and a dry ring of onion. Make the most of the wonderful range of fresh produce that is available in our shops and markets.

Steam broccoli and cabbage so that they are colorful and crunchy. Enjoy the wonderfully appetizing shades of orange and yellow bell peppers and the almost unbelievable purple-brown of eggplant. Try grating root vegetables—carrots and daikon or mooli—to add flavor and texture to garnishes and casseroles. Look for red and curly lettuces to bring excitement to an enticing summer salad. Use sweet baby tomatoes in salads and on skewers, and raid your garden and windowsill for sprigs of fresh mint and basil leaves.

Nuts and seeds are high in fat, so both should be used in moderation. However, they are a valuable source of protein and minerals, and vegetarians and vegans in particular need to ensure that their diets contain these valuable ingredients.

Vegetable Spaghetti with Lemon Dressing

Steaming vegetables helps to preserve their nutritional content and allows them to retain their bright, natural colors and crunchy texture.

Serves 4

CALORIES PER SERVING: 330 • FAT CONTENT PER SERVING: 2.5 G

INGREDIENTS

8 ounces celery root
2 medium carrots
2 medium leeks
1 small red bell pepper
1 small yellow bell pepper
2 garlic cloves
1 tsp celery seeds

1 tbsp lemon juice
10^1/$_2$ ounces spaghetti
celery leaves, chopped, to garnish

LEMON DRESSING:
1 tsp finely grated lemon rind
1 tbsp lemon juice

4 tbsp low-fat unsweetened yogurt
salt and pepper
2 tbsp snipped fresh chives

1 Peel the celery root and carrots and cut them into thin matchsticks, using a sharp knife. Place the celery root and carrots in a bowl. Trim and slice the leeks, rinse under running water to flush out any trapped dirt, then shred finely. Halve, seed and slice the bell peppers. Peel and thinly slice the garlic. Add all of the vegetables to the bowl containing the celery root and the carrots.

2 Toss the vegetables with the celery seeds and lemon juice.

3 Bring a large saucepan of water to a boil and cook the spaghetti according to the instructions on the packet. Drain and keep warm.

4 Meanwhile, bring another large saucepan of water to a boil, put the vegetables in a steamer or strainer and place over the boiling water. Cover and steam for 6–7 minutes or until tender.

5 When the spaghetti and vegetables are cooked, mix the ingredients for the lemon dressing together.

6 Transfer the spaghetti and vegetables into a warm serving bowl and mix with the dressing. Garnish with chopped celery leaves and serve.

Pesto Pasta

Italian pesto is usually laden with fat. This version has just as much flavor, but is much healthier.

Serves 4

CALORIES PER SERVING: 350 • FAT CONTENT PER SERVING: 4.5 G

INGREDIENTS

8 ounces crimini mushrooms, sliced
3/4 cup fresh vegetable stock
6 ounces asparagus, trimmed and cut
   into 2-inch lengths
10 1/2 ounces green and
   white tagliatelle
14 ounces canned artichoke hearts,
   drained and halved

bread sticks, to serve

TO GARNISH:
basil leaves, shredded
Parmesan shavings

PESTO:
2 large garlic cloves, crushed

1/2 ounce fresh basil leaves, washed
6 tbsp low-fat unsweetened yogurt
2 tbsp freshly grated
   Parmesan cheese
salt and pepper

1 Place the sliced mushrooms in a saucepan along with the stock. Bring to a boil, cover, and simmer for 3–4 minutes, until just tender. Drain and set aside, reserving the liquid to use in soups if wished.

2 Bring a small saucepan of water to a boil and cook the asparagus for 3–4 minutes, until just tender. Drain and set aside until required.

3 Bring a large pan of lightly salted water to a boil and cook the tagliatelle according to the instructions on the packet. Drain, return to the pan, and keep warm.

4 Meanwhile, make the pesto. Place all of the ingredients in a blender or food processor and process for a few seconds until smooth. Alternatively, finely chop the basil and mix all the ingredients together.

5 Add the mushrooms, asparagus, and artichoke hearts to the pasta and cook, stirring, over a low heat for 2–3 minutes. Remove from the heat, mix with the pesto, and transfer to a warm bowl. Garnish with shredded basil leaves and Parmesan shavings and serve with bread sticks.

Rice-stuffed Mushrooms

Flat mushrooms have a firm texture, which makes them ideal for baking. They are filled with the tender but more strongly flavored exotic mushrooms, although you can use ordinary varieties.

Serves 4

CALORIES PER SERVING: 315 • FAT CONTENT PER SERVING: 6 G

INGREDIENTS

4 large flat mushrooms
3^1/$_2$ ounces assorted exotic
   mushrooms
4 dry-pack, sun-dried
   tomatoes, shredded
^{2}/$_3$ cup dry red wine

4 scallions, trimmed and
   finely chopped
1^1/$_2$ cups cooked red rice
salt and pepper
2 tbsp freshly grated
   Parmesan cheese

4 thick slices granary or whole-
   wheat bread
scallion, shredded,
   to garnish

1 Preheat the oven to 375°F. Peel the flat mushrooms, pull out the stalks, and set aside. Finely chop the stalks and place in a saucepan.

2 Add the exotic mushrooms to the saucepan, along with the tomatoes and red wine. Bring to a boil, cover, and simmer gently for 2–3 minutes, until just tender. Drain, reserving the cooking liquid, and place in a small bowl.

3 Gently stir in the chopped scallions and cooked rice. Season well and stuff into the flat mushrooms, pressing the mixture down gently. Sprinkle with the grated Parmesan cheese.

4 Arrange the mushrooms in an ovenproof baking dish and pour the reserved cooking juices around them. Bake in the oven for 20–25 minutes, until they are just cooked.

5 Meanwhile, preheat the broiler. Trim the crusts from the bread and toast on each side until lightly browned.

6 Drain the mushrooms and place each one on a piece of toasted bread. Garnish with scallions and serve.

Biryani with Caramelized Onions

An assortment of vegetables cooked with tender rice, flavored and colored with bright yellow turmeric and other warming Indian spices, is served with a topping of sweet caramelized onions.

Serves 4

CALORIES PER SERVING: 365 • FAT CONTENT PER SERVING: 4.5 G

INGREDIENTS

1 cup Basmati rice, rinsed
$^1/_3$ cup red lentils, rinsed
1 bay leaf
6 cardamom pods, split
1 tsp ground turmeric
6 cloves
1 tsp cumin seeds
1 cinnamon stick, broken

1 onion, chopped
8 ounces cauliflower, broken into
   small flowerets
1 large carrot, diced
$3^1/_2$ ounces frozen peas
2 ounces golden raisins
$2^1/_2$ cups fresh vegetable stock
salt and pepper

2 tbsp chopped fresh cilantro, to
   garnish
naan bread, to serve

CARAMELIZED ONIONS:
2 tsp vegetable oil
1 medium red onion, shredded
1 medium onion, shredded
2 tsp superfine sugar

1 Place the rice, lentils, bay leaf, spices, onion, cauliflower, carrot, peas, and golden raisins in a large saucepan. Season with salt and pepper and mix well.

2 Pour in the stock, bring to a boil, cover, and simmer for 15 minutes, stirring occasionally, until the rice is tender. Remove from the heat and let stand,

covered, for 10 minutes to allow the stock to be absorbed. Discard the bay leaf, cardamom pods, cloves, and cinnamon stick.

3 Meanwhile, make the caramelized onions. Heat the oil in a skillet and sauté the onions over a medium heat for 3–4 minutes until just softened. Add the superfine sugar, raise the

heat, and cook, stirring occasionally, for a further 2–3 minutes, until the onions are just golden.

4 Gently mix the rice and vegetables and pile onto warm serving plates. Garnish with chopped cilantro, spoon the caramelized onion on top, and serve with warmed naan bread.

Soft Pancakes with Stir-fried Vegetables & Bean Curd

Chinese pancakes are made with hardly any fat—they are simply flattened white flour dough.

Serves 4

CALORIES PER SERVING: 215 • FAT CONTENT PER SERVING: 8.5 G

INGREDIENTS

1 tbsp vegetable oil
1 garlic clove, crushed
1-inch piece fresh ginger root, grated
1 bunch scallions, trimmed and
  shredded lengthwise
$3^1/_2$ ounces snow peas, topped, tailed
  and shredded
8 ounces bean curd, drained and cut
  into $^1/_2$-inch pieces

2 tbsp dark soy sauce, plus extra
  to serve
2 tbsp hoisin sauce, plus extra
  to serve
2 ounces canned bamboo
  shoots, drained
2 ounces canned water chestnuts,
  drained and sliced
$3^1/_2$ ounces bean sprouts

1 small red chili, seeded and
  thinly sliced
1 small bunch fresh chives
12 soft Chinese pancakes

TO SERVE:
shredded Chinese leaves
1 cucumber, sliced
strips of red chili

1 Heat the oil in a nonstick wok or a large skillet and stir-fry the garlic and ginger for 1 minute.

2 Add the scallions, snow peas, bean curd, soy sauce, and hoisin sauce. Stir-fry for about 2 minutes.

3 Add the bamboo shoots, water chestnuts, bean sprouts, and sliced red chili to the wok or skillet. Stir-fry gently for a further 2 minutes, until the vegetables are just tender, but still have bite. Snip the chives into 1-inch lengths and stir them into the mixture in the wok or skillet.

4 Meanwhile, heat the pancakes according to the instructions on the packet and keep warm.

5 Divide the vegetables and bean curd among the pancakes. Roll up the pancakes, and serve with the Chinese leaves and extra sauce for dipping.

Charbroiled Mediterranean Vegetable Skewers

*This medley of bell peppers, zucchini, eggplant,
and red onion can be served on its own or as an unusual side dish.*

Makes 8

CALORIES PER SERVING: 65 • FAT CONTENT PER SERVING: 2.5 G

INGREDIENTS

1 large red bell pepper
1 large green bell pepper
1 large orange bell pepper
1 large zucchini
4 baby eggplant
2 medium red onions

2 tbsp lemon juice
1 tbsp olive oil
1 garlic clove, crushed
1 tbsp chopped, fresh rosemary *or*
   1 tsp dried
salt and pepper

TO SERVE:
cracked wheat
tomato and olive relish

1 Halve and seed the bell peppers and cut into even sized pieces, about 1 inch wide. Trim the zucchini, cut in half lengthwise, and slice into 1-inch pieces. Place the bell peppers and zucchini into a large bowl and set aside.

2 Using a sharp knife, trim the eggplant and quarter them lengthwise. Peel the onions, then cut each one into 8 even-sized wedges. Add the eggplant and onion pieces to the bowl containing the bell peppers and zucchini.

3 In a small bowl, mix together the lemon juice, olive oil, garlic, rosemary, and salt and pepper to taste. Pour the mixture over the vegetables and stir well to coat.

4 Preheat the broiler. Thread the vegetables onto 8 skewers. Arrange the skewers on the rack and cook for 10–12 minutes, turning frequently, until the vegetables are lightly charred and just softened.

5 Drain the vegetable skewers and serve on a bed of cracked wheat accompanied with a tomato and olive relish, if desired.

Stuffed Vegetables Middle Eastern-style

You can fill your favorite vegetables with this nutty tasting combination of cracked wheat, tomatoes, and cucumber, with the flavors of cumin, cilantro, and mint.

Serves 4

CALORIES PER SERVING: 330 • FAT CONTENT PER SERVING: 5.5 G

INGREDIENTS

4 large beefsteak tomatoes
4 medium zucchini
2 orange bell peppers
salt and pepper

TO SERVE:
warm pita bread and low-fat hummus

FILLING:
1¼ cups cracked wheat
¼ cucumber
1 medium red onion
2 tbsp lemon juice
2 tbsp chopped fresh cilantro
2 tbsp chopped fresh mint

1 tbsp olive oil
2 tsp cumin seeds

1 Preheat the oven to 400°F. Cut off the tops from the tomatoes and reserve. Using a teaspoon, scoop out the tomato pulp, chop, and place in a bowl. Season the tomato shells, then turn them upside down on absorbent paper towels to drain thoroughly.

2 Trim the zucchini and cut a V-shaped groove lengthwise down each one. Finely chop the cut-out zucchini and add to the tomato pulp. Season the zucchini shells and set aside.

3 Halve the bell peppers. Leaving the stalks intact, cut out the seeds, and discard. Season the bell pepper shells and set aside.

4 To make the filling, soak the cracked wheat according to the instructions on the packet. Finely chop the cucumber and add to the reserved tomato pulp and zucchini mixture.

5 Finely chop the onion, and add to the vegetable mixture with the lemon juice, herbs, olive oil, cumin, and seasoning, and mix together well.

6 When the wheat has soaked, mix with the vegetables and stuff into the tomato, zucchini and bell pepper shells. Place the tops on the tomatoes, transfer to a roasting pan and bake for 20–25 minutes, until cooked through. Drain and serve.

Fragrant Asparagus & Orange Risotto

Soft, creamy rice combines with the flavors of citrus and light aniseed to make this delicious supper for four or a substantial starter for six.

Serves 4–6

CALORIES PER SERVING: 420–280 • FAT CONTENT PER SERVING: 7.5–5 G

INGREDIENTS

4 ounces fine asparagus
  spears, trimmed
5 cups vegetable stock
2 bulbs fennel
1 ounce low-fat spread

1 tsp olive oil
2 celery stalks, trimmed and chopped
2 medium leeks, trimmed
  and shredded
2 cups arborio rice

3 medium oranges
salt and pepper

1 Bring a small saucepan of water to a boil and cook the asparagus for 1 minute. Drain and set aside.

2 Pour the stock into a saucepan and bring to a boil. Reduce the heat to maintain a gentle simmer.

3 Meanwhile, trim the fennel, reserving the fronds, and cut into thin slices. Carefully melt the low-fat spread with the oil in a large saucepan, taking care that the water in the low-fat spread does not evaporate, and gently sauté the fennel, celery, and leeks for 3–4 minutes, until just softened. Add the rice and cook, stirring, for a further 2 minutes, until mixed.

4 Add a ladleful of stock to the pan and cook gently, stirring, until absorbed. Continue ladling the stock into the rice until the rice becomes creamy, thick, and tender. This process will take about 25 minutes and should not be hurried.

5 Finely grate the rind and extract the juice from 1 orange and mix into the rice. Carefully remove the peel and pith from the remaining oranges. Holding the fruit over the saucepan, cut out the orange segments and add to the rice, along with any juice that falls.

6 Stir the orange into the rice, along with the asparagus spears. Season with salt and pepper, garnish with the reserved fennel fronds, and serve.

Spicy Black Eye Peas

A hearty casserole of black eye peas in a rich, sweet tomato sauce flavored with molasses and mustard. It is ideal served with crusty bread to mop up the sauce.

Serves 4

CALORIES PER SERVING: 445 • FAT CONTENT PER SERVING: 6 G

INGREDIENTS

2 cups black eye peas, soaked
   overnight in cold water
1 tbsp vegetable oil
2 medium onions, chopped
1 tbsp clear honey
2 tbsp molasses
4 tbsp dark soy sauce
1 tsp dry mustard powder

4 tbsp tomato paste
2 cups fresh vegetable stock
1 bay leaf
1 sprig each of rosemary, thyme,
   and sage
1 small orange
pepper
1 tbsp cornstarch

2 medium red bell peppers, seeded
   and diced
2 tbsp chopped fresh parsley,
   to garnish
crusty bread, to serve

1 Preheat the oven to 300°F. Rinse the peas and place in a saucepan. Cover with water, bring to a boil, and boil rapidly for 10 minutes. Drain and place in an ovenproof casserole dish.

2 Meanwhile, heat the oil in a skillet and sauté the onions for 5 minutes. Stir in the honey, molasses, soy sauce, mustard, and tomato paste. Pour in the stock,

bring to a boil, and pour over the peas.

3 Tie the bay leaf and herbs together with a clean piece of string and add to the pan containing the peas. Using a vegetable peeler, pare off 3 pieces of orange rind and mix into the peas, along with plenty of freshly ground black pepper. Cover and bake for about 1 hour.

4 Extract the juice from the orange and blend with the cornstarch to form a paste. Stir into the peas, along with the red bell peppers. Cover and cook for 1 hour, until the sauce is rich and thick and the peas are tender. Discard the herbs and orange rind.

5 Garnish with chopped parsley and serve with lots of fresh crusty bread.

Mexican-style Pizzas

Ready-made pizza bases are covered with a chili-flavored tomato sauce and topped with kidney beans, cheese, and jalapeño chilies in this blend of American, Italian, and Mexican cooking.

Serves 4

CALORIES PER SERVING: 585 • FAT CONTENT PER SERVING: 16 G

INGREDIENTS

4 ready-made individual
  pizza bases
1 tbsp olive oil
7 ounce can chopped tomatoes with
  garlic and herbs
2 tbsp tomato paste

7 ounce can kidney beans, drained
  and rinsed
4 ounces corn kernels, thawed
  if frozen
1–2 tsp chili sauce
1 large red onion, shredded

3$\frac{1}{2}$ ounces reduced-fat cheddar
  cheese, grated
1 large green chili, sliced into rings
2 tbsp fresh cilantro, chopped
salt and pepper

1 Preheat the oven to 425°F. Arrange the pizza bases on a cookie sheet and brush them lightly with the oil.

2 In a bowl, mix together the chopped tomatoes, tomato paste, kidney beans, and corn, and add chili sauce to taste. Season with salt and pepper.

3 Spread the tomato and kidney bean mixture evenly over each pizza base to cover. Top each pizza with shredded onion and sprinkle with some grated cheese and a few slices of green chili according to taste. Bake in the oven for about 20 minutes until the vegetables are tender, the cheese has melted, and the base is crisp and golden.

4 Remove the pizzas from the cookie sheet and transfer to serving plates. Sprinkle with chopped cilantro and serve immediately.

COOK'S TIP

For a low-fat Mexican-style salad to serve with this pizza, arrange sliced tomatoes, fresh cilantro leaves, and a few slices of a small, ripe avocado. Sprinkle with fresh lime juice and coarse sea salt. Avocados have quite a high oil content, so eat in moderation.

Eggplant Pasta Cake

This dish would make a stunning dinner party dish, yet it contains simple ingredients and is easy to make. The "cake" would serve six as a main course or eight as a filling starter.

Serves 6–8

CALORIES PER SERVING: 290–215 • FAT CONTENT PER SERVING: 7–5 G

INGREDIENTS

1 medium eggplant
10^1/2 ounces tricolor pasta shapes
4 ounces low-fat soft cheese with
   garlic and herbs

1^1/3 cups sieved tomatoes
4 tbsp grated Parmesan cheese
1^1/2 tsp dried oregano
2 tbsp dry white breadcrumbs

salt and pepper

1 Preheat the oven to 375°F. Grease and line an 8 inch round spring-form cake pan.

2 Trim the eggplant and slice lengthwise into slices about ¼ inch thick. Place in a bowl, sprinkle with salt, and set aside for 30 minutes to remove any bitter juices. Rinse well under cold running water and drain.

3 Bring a saucepan of water to a boil and blanch the eggplant slices for 1 minute. Drain and pat dry with paper towels. Set aside.

4 Cook the pasta shapes according to the instructions on the packet; for best results, the pasta should be slightly undercooked. Drain well and return to the saucepan. Add the soft cheese and allow it to melt over the pasta.

5 Stir in the sieved tomatoes, Parmesan cheese, oregano, and seasoning. Set aside.

6 Arrange the eggplant over the base and sides of the prepared cake pan, overlapping the slices and making sure there are no gaps between them.

7 Pile the pasta mixture into the pan, packing down well, and sprinkle with the breadcrumbs. Bake for 20 minutes and let stand for 15 minutes.

8 Loosen the cake around the edge with a spatula and release from the pan. Turn out eggplant-side up and serve hot.

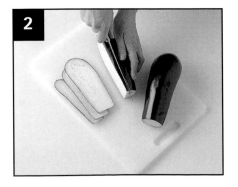

Mushroom Cannelloni

Thick pasta tubes are filled with a mixture of seasoned chopped mushrooms, and baked in a rich fragrant tomato sauce. Serve with shavings of Parmesan, if desired.

Serves 4

CALORIES PER SERVING: 315 • FAT CONTENT PER SERVING: 3.5 G

INGREDIENTS

12 ounces crimini mushrooms, finely chopped
1 medium onion, finely chopped
1 garlic clove, crushed
1 tbsp chopped fresh thyme
1/2 tsp ground nutmeg
4 tbsp dry white wine
4 tbsp fresh white breadcrumbs

12 dried "quick-cook" cannelloni
salt and pepper
1 ounce piece Parmesan cheese, to garnish (optional)

TOMATO SAUCE:
1 large red bell pepper
3/4 cup dry white wine
2 cups sieved tomatoes
2 tbsp tomato paste
2 bay leaves
1 tsp superfine sugar

1 Preheat the oven to 400°F. Place the mushrooms, onion, and garlic in a pan. Stir in the thyme, nutmeg, and 4 tbsp wine. Bring to a boil, cover, and simmer for 10 minutes.

2 Stir in the breadcrumbs to bind the mixture together and season. Cool for 10 minutes.

3 Preheat the broiler. To make the sauce, halve and seed the bell pepper, place on the broiler rack, and cook for 8–10 minutes, until charred. Let cool for 10 minutes.

4 Once the bell pepper has cooled, peel off the charred skin. Chop the flesh and place in a food processor with the wine. Blend until smooth, and pour into a pan.

5 Mix the remaining sauce ingredients with the bell pepper and wine and season. Bring to a boil and simmer for 10 minutes. Discard the bay leaves.

6 Cover the base of an ovenproof dish with a thin layer of sauce. Fill the cannelloni with the mushroom mixture and place in the dish. Spoon the remaining sauce on top, cover with foil, and bake for 35–40 minutes. Garnish with Parmesan shavings (if using) and serve.

Bean Curd & Garbanzo Burgers

Flavored with spices, these burgers are delicious served with a tahini-flavored relish.

Serves 4

CALORIES PER SERVING: 280 • FAT CONTENT PER SERVING: 9 G

INGREDIENTS

1 small red onion, finely chopped
1 garlic clove, crushed
1 tsp ground cumin
1 tsp ground coriander
2 tbsp lemon juice
15 ounce can garbanzo beans,
    drained and rinsed
3 ounces soft silken bean
    curd, drained
4 ounces cooked potato, diced

4 tbsp freshly chopped cilantro
2 tbsp all-purpose flour (optional)
$2^3/_4$ ounces dry brown breadcrumbs
1 tbsp vegetable oil
burger rolls
2 medium tomatoes, sliced
1 large carrot, grated
salt and pepper

RELISH:
1 tsp tahini paste
4 tbsp low-fat unsweetened yogurt
1-inch piece cucumber,
    finely chopped
1 tbsp chopped, fresh cilantro
garlic salt, to season

1 Place the onion, garlic, spices, and lemon juice in a pan, bring to a boil, cover, and simmer for 5 minutes until softened.

2 Place the garbanzo beans, bean curd, and potato in a bowl and mash well. Stir in the onion mixture, cilantro, and seasoning, and mix together. Divide into 4 equal portions and form into patties 4 inches across, dusting the hands with flour, if necessary.

3 Sprinkle the breadcrumbs onto a plate and press the burgers into the crumbs to coat both sides.

4 Heat the oil in a large nonstick skillet and fry the burgers for 5 minutes on each side, until heated through and golden. Drain on paper towels.

5 Meanwhile, mix all of the relish ingredients together in a bowl and chill.

6 Line the rolls with tomato and grated carrot and top each with a burger. Serve with the relish.

Sweet Potato & Leek Patties

Sweet potatoes have very dense flesh and a delicious, sweet, earthy taste.

Serves 4

CALORIES PER SERVING: 385 • FAT CONTENT PER SERVING: 6.5 G

INGREDIENTS

2 pounds sweet potato

4 tsp sunflower oil

2 medium leeks, trimmed and
   finely chopped

1 garlic clove, crushed

1-inch piece fresh ginger root,
   finely chopped

7 ounce can corn kernels, drained

2 tbsp low-fat unsweetened yogurt

2 ounces whole-wheat flour

salt and pepper

GINGER SAUCE:

2 tbsp white wine vinegar

2 tsp superfine sugar

1 red chili, seeded and chopped

1-inch piece fresh ginger root, cut
   into thin strips

2 tbsp ginger wine

4 tbsp fresh vegetable stock

1 tsp cornstarch

TO SERVE:

lettuce leaves

scallions

1 Peel the potatoes and cut into ¾-inch thick pieces. Place in a saucepan, cover with water, and boil for 10–15 minutes. Drain well and mash. Let cool.

2 Heat 2 tsp of oil and sauté the leeks, garlic, and chopped ginger for 2–3 minutes.

3 Stir the leek mixture into the potato with the corn, seasoning, and unsweetened yogurt. Form into 8 patties and toss in flour to coat on both sides. Chill for 30 minutes.

4 Preheat the broiler. Place the patties on a broiler rack and lightly brush with oil. Broil for 5 minutes, then turn over. Brush with oil and broil for a further 5 minutes, until golden. Drain on paper towels.

5 To make the sauce, place the vinegar, sugar, chili, and ginger in a pan. Bring to a boil and simmer for 5 minutes. Stir in the ginger wine. Blend the stock and cornstarch to form a paste and stir into the sauce. Heat through, stirring, until thickened.

6 Transfer the patties to serving plates, spoon the sauce over the patties, and serve immediately.

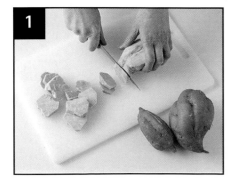

Ratatouille Vegetable Broil

Ratatouille is a French classic—a sumptuous dish of vegetables cooked in a tomato and herb sauce. Here it has a topping of diced potatoes and a golden layer of cheese.

Serves 4

CALORIES PER SERVING: 330 • FAT CONTENT PER SERVING: 4 G

INGREDIENTS

2 medium onions
1 garlic clove
1 medium red bell pepper
1 medium green bell pepper
1 medium eggplant

2 medium zucchini
2 x 14 ounce cans chopped tomatoes
1 bouquet garni
2 tbsp tomato paste
2 pounds potatoes

$2^3/4$ ounces reduced-fat cheddar
  cheese, grated
salt and pepper
2 tbsp snipped fresh chives, to garnish

1 Peel and finely chop the onions and garlic. Rinse, seed, and slice the bell peppers. Rinse, trim, and cut the eggplant into small dice. Rinse, trim, and thinly slice the zucchini.

2 Place the onion, garlic, and bell peppers into a large pan. Add the tomatoes and stir in the bouquet garni, tomato paste, and salt and pepper. Bring to a boil, cover, and simmer for 10 minutes, stirring halfway through.

3 Stir in the prepared eggplant and zucchini and cook, uncovered, for a further 10 minutes, stirring the mixture occasionally.

4 Meanwhile, peel the potatoes and cut into 1-inch cubes. Place the potatoes into another saucepan and cover with water. Bring to a boil and cook for 10–12 minutes, until tender. Drain thoroughly with a slotted spoon and set aside.

5 Transfer the vegetables to a heatproof gratin dish. Pile the cooked potato cubes evenly over the vegetables.

6 Preheat the broiler. Sprinkle grated cheese over the potatoes and place under the broiler for 5 minutes until golden, bubbling, and hot. Serve immediately garnished with snipped chives.

Mussel & Red Bell Pepper Salad

A colorful combination of cooked mussels tossed together with charbroiled red bell peppers, radicchio, and arugula, and a lemon and chive dressing. It makes a delicious main meal.

Serves 4

CALORIES PER SERVING: 175 • FAT CONTENT PER SERVING: 6 G

INGREDIENTS

2 large red bell peppers
12 ounces cooked shelled mussels, thawed if frozen
1 head of radicchio
1 ounce arugula leaves
8 cooked New Zealand mussels in their shells

TO SERVE:
lemon wedges
crusty bread

DRESSING:
1 tbsp olive oil
1 tbsp lemon juice

1 tsp finely grated lemon rind
2 tsp clear honey
1 tsp French mustard
1 tbsp snipped fresh chives
salt and pepper

1 Preheat the broiler. Halve and seed the bell peppers and place them skin side up on the rack. Cook for 8–10 minutes, until the skin is charred and blistered and the flesh is soft. Let cool for 10 minutes, then peel off the skin.

2 Slice the bell pepper flesh into thin strips and place in a bowl. Gently mix in the shelled mussels and set aside.

3 To make the dressing, mix all of the ingredients until well blended. Mix into the bell pepper and mussel mixture until coated.

4 Remove the central core of the radicchio and shred the leaves. Place in a serving bowl with the arugula leaves and toss together.

5 Pile the mussel mixture into the center of the leaves and arrange the large mussels around the edge of the dish. Serve with lemon wedges and crusty bread.

VARIATION

Replace the shelled mussels with peeled shrimp and the New Zealand mussels with large crevettes, if you prefer. Lime could be used instead of lemon for a different citrus flavor.

Sweet & Sour Fish Salad

This refreshing blend of pink and white fish mixed with fresh pineapple and bell peppers would make an interesting starter or a light meal.

Serves 4

CALORIES PER SERVING: 190 • FAT CONTENT PER SERVING: 7 G

INGREDIENTS

8 ounces trout fillets
8 ounces white fish fillets (such as
  haddock or cod)
1¼ cups water
1 stalk lemon grass
2 lime leaves
1 large red chili
1 bunch scallions, trimmed
  and shredded

4 ounces fresh pineapple
  flesh, diced
1 small red bell pepper, seeded
  and diced
1 bunch watercress, washed
  and trimmed
fresh snipped chives, to garnish

DRESSING:
1 tbsp sunflower oil
1 tbsp rice wine vinegar
pinch of chili powder
1 tsp clear honey
salt and pepper

1 Rinse the fish, place in a skillet, and add the water. Bend the lemon grass in half to bruise it and add to the pan with the lime leaves. Prick the chili with a fork and add to the pan. Bring to a boil and simmer for 7–8 minutes. Let cool.

2 Drain the fish fillet, flake the flesh away from the skin, and place in a bowl. Gently stir in the scallions, pineapple, and bell pepper.

3 Arrange the washed watercress on 4 serving plates, pile the cooked fish mixture on top, and set aside.

4 To make the dressing, mix all the ingredients together and season well. Spoon over the fish and serve garnished with chives.

VARIATION

This recipe also works very well if you replace the fish with 12 ounces white crabmeat. Add a dash of Tabasco sauce if you like it hot!

Beef & Peanut Salad

Although peanuts are very high in fat, they do have a strong flavor, so you can make a little go a long way. This recipe looks stunning if you arrange the ingredients rather than toss them together.

Serves 4

CALORIES PER SERVING: 320 • FAT CONTENT PER SERVING: 14 G

INGREDIENTS

$^1/_2$ head Chinese leaves
1 large carrot
4 ounces radishes
$3^1/_2$ ounces baby corn cobs
1 tbsp ground nut oil
1 red chili, seeded and
   finely chopped

1 clove garlic, finely chopped
12 ounces lean beef (such as fillet,
   sirloin, or rump), trimmed and
   finely shredded
1 tbsp dark soy sauce
1 ounce fresh peanuts (optional)
red chili, sliced, to garnish

DRESSING:
1 tbsp smooth peanut butter
1 tsp superfine sugar
2 tbsp light soy sauce
1 tbsp sherry vinegar
salt and pepper

1 Finely shred the Chinese leaves and arrange on a platter. Peel the carrot and cut into thin, matchstick-like strips. Wash, trim, and quarter the radishes, and halve the baby corn lengthwise. Arrange these ingredients around the edge of the dish and set aside.

2 Heat the oil in a nonstick wok or large skillet and stir-fry the chili, garlic, and beef for 5 minutes. Add the dark soy sauce and stir-fry for a further 1–2 minutes until tender and cooked through.

3 Meanwhile, make the dressing. Place all of the ingredients in a small bowl and blend them together until smooth.

4 Place the hot cooked beef in the center of the salad ingredients. Spoon over the dressing and sprinkle with a few peanuts, if using. Garnish with slices of red chili and serve the salad immediately.

VARIATION

If preferred, use chicken, turkey, lean pork, or even strips of venison instead of beef in this recipe. Cut off all visible fat before you begin.

Chicken & Spinach Salad

A simple combination of lean chicken with fresh young spinach leaves and a few fresh raspberries is served with a refreshing yogurt and honey dressing. This recipe is perfect for a summer lunch.

Serves 4

CALORIES PER SERVING: 225 • FAT CONTENT PER SERVING: 6 G

INGREDIENTS

4 boneless, skinless chicken breasts, 5¹/₂ ounces each
2 cups fresh chicken stock
1 bay leaf
8 ounces fresh young spinach leaves
1 small red onion, shredded

4 ounces fresh raspberries
salt and freshly ground pink peppercorns
fresh toasted croûtons, to garnish

DRESSING:
4 tbsp low-fat unsweetened yogurt
1 tbsp raspberry vinegar
2 tsp clear honey

1 Place the chicken breasts in a skillet. Add the stock and the bay leaf. Bring to a boil, cover, and simmer for 15–20 minutes, turning halfway through, until the chicken is cooked through. Allow to cool in the liquid.

2 Arrange the spinach on 4 serving plates and top with the onion. Cover and chill in the refrigerator.

3 Drain the cooked chicken and pat dry on absorbent paper towels. Slice the chicken breasts thinly and arrange, fanned out, over the spinach and onion. Sprinkle with the raspberries.

4 To make the dressing, mix all the ingredients together in a small bowl. Drizzle a spoonful of dressing over each chicken breast and season with salt and ground

pink peppercorns to taste. Serve with freshly toasted croûtons.

VARIATION

This recipe is delicious with smoked chicken, but it will be more expensive and richer, so use slightly less. It would make an impressive starter for a dinner party.

Pasta Provençale

A combination of Mediterranean vegetables tossed in a tomato dressing, served on a bed of assorted salad greens, makes a tasty main meal or an appetizing side dish.

Serves 4

CALORIES PER SERVING: 295 • FAT CONTENT PER SERVING: 6 G

INGREDIENTS

8 ounces penne (pasta quills)
1 tbsp olive oil
1 ounce pitted black olives, drained and chopped
1 ounce dry-pack sun-dried tomatoes, soaked, drained, and chopped
3¹/₂ ounces assorted baby salad greens

14 ounce can artichoke hearts, drained and halved
4 ounces baby zucchini, trimmed and sliced
4 ounces baby plum tomatoes, halved
salt and pepper
shredded basil leaves, to garnish

DRESSING:
4 tbsp sieved tomatoes
2 tbsp low-fat unsweetened yogurt
1 tbsp unsweetened orange juice
1 small bunch fresh basil, shredded

1 Cook the penne (pasta quills) according to the instructions on the packet. Do not overcook the pasta—it should still have bite. Drain well and return to the pan. Stir in the olive oil, salt and pepper, olives, and sun-dried tomatoes. Let cool.

2 Gently mix the artichokes, zucchini, and plum tomatoes into the cooked pasta. Arrange the salad greens in a serving bowl.

3 To make the dressing, mix all of the ingredients together until well combined and toss into the vegetables and pasta.

4 Spoon the mixture on top of the salad greens and garnish with shredded basil leaves.

VARIATION

For a nonvegetarian version, stir 8 ounces canned tuna in brine, drained, and flaked, into the pasta together with the vegetables. Other pasta shapes can be included—try farfalle (bows) and rotelle (spoked wheels).

Root Vegetable Salad

This colorful salad of grated vegetables is perfect for a light starter.
The peppery flavors of the daikon and radishes are refreshingly pungent.
Serve with some toasted bread and assorted salad greens.

Serves 4

CALORIES PER SERVING: 150 • FAT CONTENT PER SERVING: 9 G

INGREDIENTS

12 ounces carrots

8 ounces daikon (white radish)

4 ounces radishes

12 ounces celery root

1 tbsp orange juice

2 celery stalks with leaves, washed
  and trimmed

3$^1/_2$ ounces assorted salad greens

1 ounce walnut pieces

DRESSING:

1 tbsp walnut oil

1 tbsp white wine vinegar

1 tsp wholegrain mustard

$^1/_2$ tsp finely grated orange rind

1 tsp celery seeds

salt and pepper

---

1 Peel and coarsely grate or very finely shred the carrots, daikon, and radishes. Set aside in separate bowls.

2 Peel and coarsely grate or finely shred the celery root and mix with the orange juice.

3 Remove the celery leaves and reserve. Finely chop the celery stalks.

4 Divide the salad greens among 4 serving plates and arrange the vegetables in small piles on top. Set aside while you make the dressing.

5 Mix all of the dressing ingredients together and season well. Drizzle a little over each salad. Shred the reserved celery leaves and sprinkle over the salad with the walnut pieces.

COOK'S TIP

Also known as Chinese white radish and mooli, daikon resembles a large white parsnip. It has crisp, slightly pungent flesh, which can be eaten raw or cooked. It is a useful ingredient in stir-fries. Fresh daikon tend to have a stronger flavor than store-bought ones.

Beet & Orange Rice Salad

You must use freshly cooked beet in this unusual combination of colors and flavors. Beet that has been soaked in vinegar will spoil the delicate balance.

Serves 4

CALORIES PER SERVING: 335 • FAT CONTENT PER SERVING: 2.5 G

INGREDIENTS

1^1/$_3$ cups long-grain and wild rices (see Cook's Tip)

4 large oranges

1 pound cooked beet, peeled

2 heads of chicory

salt and pepper

fresh snipped chives, to garnish

DRESSING:

4 tbsp low-fat unsweetened yogurt

1 garlic clove, crushed

1 tbsp wholegrain mustard

^{1}/$_2$ tsp finely grated orange rind

2 tsp clear honey

1 Cook the rices according to the instructions on the packet. Drain and set aside to cool.

2 Meanwhile, slice the top and bottom off each orange. Using a sharp knife, remove the skin and pith. Holding the orange over a bowl to catch the juice, carefully slice between each segment. Place the segments in a separate bowl. Cover the juice and chill in the refrigerator until required.

3 Drain the beet if necessary and dice into cubes. Mix with the orange segments, cover, and leave to chill.

4 When the rice has cooled, mix in the reserved orange juice and season with salt and pepper to taste.

5 Line 4 serving bowls or plates with the chicory leaves. Spoon the rice over the leaves and top with the beet and oranges.

6 Mix all the dressing ingredients together and spoon over the salad, or serve separately in a bowl, if preferred. Garnish with fresh snipped chives.

COOK'S TIP

Look for boxes of ready-mixed long-grain and wild rices. Alternatively, you can cook 1 cup white rice and ^{1}/$_4$ cup wild rice separately.

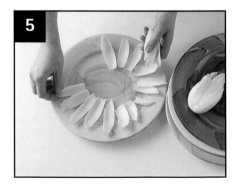

Red Hot Slaw

Red in color and red-hot in taste, too—just how much chili powder you add is up to you.
As well as being an exciting side dish, this salad makes a good filling for baked potatoes.

Serves 4

CALORIES PER SERVING: 200 • FAT CONTENT PER SERVING: 8.5 G

INGREDIENTS

¹/₂ small red cabbage
1 large carrot
2 red-skinned apples
1 tbsp lemon juice
1 medium red onion
3¹/₂ ounces reduced-fat Cheddar
cheese, grated

TO GARNISH:
red chili strips
carrot strips

DRESSING:
3 tbsp reduced-calorie mayonnaise
3 tbsp low-fat unsweetened yogurt
1 garlic clove, crushed

1 tsp paprika
1–2 tsp chili powder
pinch cayenne pepper (optional)
salt and pepper

1 Cut the red cabbage in half and remove the central core. Finely shred the leaves and place in a large bowl. Peel and coarsely grate or finely shred the carrot and mix into the cabbage.

2 Core the apples and finely dice, leaving on the skins. Place in another bowl and toss in the lemon juice to help prevent the apple from browning. Mix the apple into the cabbage and carrot.

3 Peel and finely shred or grate the onion. Stir into the other vegetables, along with the cheese, and mix together.

4 To make the dressing, mix together the mayonnaise, yogurt, garlic, and paprika in a small bowl. Add chili powder according to taste, and the cayenne pepper, if using—remember this will add more spice to the dressing. Season well.

5 Toss the dressing into the vegetables and mix well. Cover and chill in the refrigerator for 1 hour to allow the flavors to develop. Serve garnished with strips of red chili and carrot.

Pasta Niçoise Salad

Based on the classic French salad niçoise, this recipe contains pasta instead of potatoes.
The very light olive oil dressing has the tang of capers and the fragrance of fresh basil.

Serves 4

CALORIES PER SERVING: 370 • FAT CONTENT PER SERVING: 9 G

INGREDIENTS

8 ounces farfalle (pasta bows)
6 ounces green beans, topped
  and tailed
12 ounces fresh tuna steaks
4 ounces baby plum
  tomatoes, halved
8 anchovy fillets, drained on
  absorbent paper towels

2 tbsp capers in brine, drained
1 ounce pitted black olives in
  brine, drained
fresh basil leaves, to garnish
salt and pepper

DRESSING:
1 tbsp olive oil
1 garlic clove, crushed
1 tbsp lemon juice
$1/2$ tsp finely grated lemon rind
1 tbsp shredded fresh basil leaves

1 Cook the pasta in lightly salted boiling water according to the instructions on the packet until just cooked. Drain well, set aside and keep warm.

2 Bring a small saucepan of lightly salted water to a boil and cook the green beans for 5–6 minutes, until just tender. Drain well and toss into the pasta. Set aside and keep warm.

3 Preheat the broiler. Rinse and pat the tuna steaks dry on absorbent paper towels. Season on both sides with black pepper. Place the tuna steaks on the broiler rack and cook for 4–5 minutes on each side, until cooked through.

4 Drain the tuna on absorbent paper towels and flake into bite-size pieces. Toss the tuna into the pasta, along with the tomatoes, anchovies, capers, and olives. Set aside and keep warm.

5 Meanwhile, prepare the dressing. Mix all the ingredients together and season well. Pour the dressing over the pasta mixture and mix carefully. Transfer to a warmed serving bowl and serve sprinkled with fresh basil leaves.

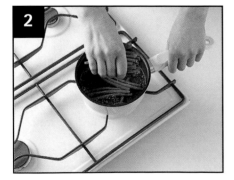

Coconut Couscous Salad

The nutty taste of toasted coconut really stands out in this delicious dish, which can also be served hot, without the dressing, to accompany a rich lamb stew.

Serves 4

CALORIES PER SERVING: 270 • FAT CONTENT PER SERVING: 10 G

INGREDIENTS

12 ounces couscous
6 ounces dried apricots
1 small bunch fresh chives
2 tbsp unsweetened
  shredded coconut
1 tsp ground cinnamon

salt and pepper
mint leaves, to garnish

DRESSING:
1 tbsp olive oil
2 tbsp unsweetened orange juice

$^{1}/_{2}$ tsp finely grated orange rind
1 tsp wholegrain mustard
1 tsp clear honey
2 tbsp chopped fresh mint leaves

1 Soak the couscous according to the instructions on the packet. Bring a large saucepan of water to a boil. Transfer the couscous to a steamer or large strainer lined with cheesecloth and place over the water. Cover and steam as directed. Remove from the heat, place in heatproof bowl, and set aside to cool.

2 Meanwhile, slice the apricots into thin strips and place in a small bowl. Using kitchen scissors, snip the chives over the apricots.

3 When the couscous is cool, mix in the apricots, chives, coconut, and cinnamon. Season well.

4 To make the dressing, mix all the ingredients together and season. Pour over the couscous and mix until well combined. Cover and leave to chill for 1 hour to allow the flavors to develop. Serve garnished with mint leaves.

COOK'S TIP

To serve this salad hot, when the couscous has been steamed, mix in the apricots, chives, coconut, cinnamon, and seasoning, along with 1 tbsp olive oil. Pile into a warmed serving bowl and serve.

Baking & Desserts

The ideal ending to a meal is fresh fruit, topped with low-fat yogurt. Fruit contains no fat and is sweet enough not to need extra sugar, but it is a valuable source of vitamins and fiber—ideal in every way for anyone who cares about their own and their family's health.

There are, however, dozens of other ways in which fruit can be used as the basis for desserts and bakes, and thanks to modern transportation systems, the range of unusual and exotic fruits available in supermarkets seems to expand every week. Experiment with some of these unfamiliar fruits in delicious warm desserts, sophisticated mousses and fools, and satisfying cakes, and use old favorites in enticing new ways.

From an elegant Strawberry Roulade to add the perfect finishing touch to a dinner party to a deliciously moist Carrot & Ginger Cake to offer to unexpected guests, you will find the perfect recipe for every occasion on the following pages.

Paper-thin Fruit Pies

The extra-crisp pastry cases, filled with slices of apple and pear and glazed with apricot preserve, are best served hot with low-fat custard or low-fat fruit yogurt.

Serves 4

CALORIES PER SERVING: 185 • FAT CONTENT: 7.5 G

INGREDIENTS

1 medium eating apple
1 medium ripe pear
2 tbsp lemon juice
2 ounces low-fat spread

4 rectangular sheets of filo pastry,
 thawed if frozen
2 tbsp low-sugar apricot preserve
1 tbsp unsweetened orange juice

1 tbsp finely chopped natural
 pistachio nuts
2 tsp confectioner's sugar,
 for dusting
low-fat custard, to serve

1 Preheat the oven to 400°F. Core and thinly slice the apple and pear and toss them in the lemon juice.

2 Gently melt the low-fat spread in a pan set over a low heat.

3 Cut the sheets of pastry into 4 and cover with a clean, damp dish cloth. Brush 4 nonstick large muffin pans, measuring 4 inches across, with a little of the low-fat spread.

4 Working on each pie, separately, brush 4 sheets of pastry with low-fat spread. Press a small sheet of pastry into the base of one pan. Arrange the other sheets of pastry on top at slightly different angles. Repeat with the other sheets of pastry to make another 3 pies.

5 Arrange the apple and pear slices alternately in the center of each pastry case and lightly crimp the edges of the pastry of each pie.

6 Mix the preserve and orange juice together until smooth and brush over the fruit. Bake for 12–15 minutes. Sprinkle the nuts, dust lightly with confectioner's sugar, and serve hot with low-fat custard.

VARIATION

Other combinations of fruit are equally delicious. Try peach and apricot, raspberry and apple, or pineapple and mango.

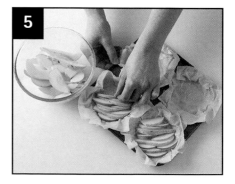

Almond Trifles

Amaretti cookies can be made with ground almonds, which give them a high fat content. For this recipe, make sure you use the cookies made from apricot kernels, which have a lower fat content.

Serves 4

CALORIES PER SERVING: 230 • FAT CONTENT PER SERVING: 3.5 G

INGREDIENTS

8 Amaretti di Saronno cookies
4 tbsp brandy *or* Amaretto liqueur
8 ounces raspberries, thawed
   if frozen
1¼ cups low-fat custard

1¼ cups low-fat unsweetened
   yogurt
1 tsp almond extract

½ ounce toasted

almonds, slivered
1 tsp cocoa powder

1 Using a rolling pin, carefully crush the cookies into small pieces.

2 Divide the crushed cookies among 4 serving glasses. Sprinkle in the brandy or liqueur and let stand for about 30 minutes to allow the cookies to soften.

3 Top the layer of cookies with a layer of raspberries, reserving a few raspberries for decoration, and spoon over enough custard to just cover.

4 Mix the unsweetened yogurt with the almond extract and spoon over the custard. Chill in the refrigerator for about 30 minutes.

5 Just before serving, sprinkle with the toasted slivered almonds and dust with a little cocoa powder. Decorate with the reserved raspberries and serve at once.

VARIATION

Try this trifle with assorted summer fruits. If they are a frozen mix, use them frozen and allow them to thaw so that the juices soak into the cookie base—it will taste delicious.

Cheese Hearts with Strawberry Sauce

These little molds look very attractive when they are made in the French coeur à la crème china molds, but you could make them in small ramekins instead.

Serves 4

CALORIES PER SERVING: 120 • FAT CONTENT PER SERVING: 0.6 G

INGREDIENTS

15^{1}/$_{2}$ ounces low-fat cottage cheese
^{2}/$_{3}$ cup low-fat unsweetened yogurt
1 medium egg white
2 tbsp superfine sugar

1–2 tsp vanilla extract
rose-scented geranium leaves,
   to decorate

SAUCE:
8 ounces strawberries
4 tbsp unsweetened orange juice
2–3 tsp confectioner's sugar

1 Line 4 heart-shaped molds or ramekins with clean cheesecloth. Place strainer over a mixing bowl and using the back of a metal spoon, press the cottage cheese through. Mix in the yogurt.

2 Whisk the egg white until stiff. Fold into the cheeses, with the superfine sugar and vanilla extract.

3 Spoon the cheese mixture into the molds and smooth over the tops. Place on a wire rack over a tray and chill for 1 hour, until firm and drained.

4 Meanwhile, make the sauce. Wash the strawberries under cold running water. Reserving a few strawberries for decoration, hull and chop the remainder. Place the strawberries in a blender or food processor with the orange juice and process until smooth. Alternatively, push through a strainer to purée. Mix with the confectioner's sugar to taste. Cover and chill until the sauce is required.

5 Remove the cheese hearts from the molds and transfer to serving plates. Remove the cheesecloth, decorate with strawberries and geranium leaves, and serve with the sauce.

COOK'S TIP

The coeur à la crème molds have drainage holes in them, so if you use ordinary ramekins or other small molds, the hearts will be much softer.

Almond & Raisin Cheesecakes

These creamy cheese desserts are so delicious that they are sure to become firm favorites—and it's hard to believe that they are low in fat.

Serves 4

CALORIES PER SERVING: 315 • FAT CONTENT PER SERVING: 16 G

INGREDIENTS

12 Amaretti di Saronno cookies
1 medium egg white, lightly beaten
8 ounces skimmed-milk soft cheese
1/2 tsp almond extract
1/2 tsp finely grated lime rind
1 ounce ground almonds

1 ounce superfine sugar
2 ounces golden raisins
2 tsp powdered gelatin
2 tbsp boiling water
2 tbsp lime juice

TO DECORATE:
1 ounces slivered toasted almonds
sliced lime

1 Preheat the oven to 350°F. Place the cookies in a clean plastic bag, seal the bag, and using a rolling pin, crush them into small pieces. Place the crumbs in a bowl and bind together with the egg white.

2 Arrange 4 nonstick pastry rings or poached egg rings, 3½ inches across, on a cookie sheet lined with baking parchment. Divide the cookie mixture into 4 equal portions and spoon it into the rings, pressing down well. Bake for 10 minutes, until crisp, and allow to cool in the rings.

3 Beat together the soft cheese, almond extract, lime rind, ground almonds, sugar, and golden raisins until well mixed.

4 Dissolve the gelatin in the boiling water and stir in the lime juice. Fold into the cheese mixture and spoon over the cookie bases. Smooth over the tops and chill for 1 hour, or until set.

5 Loosen the cheesecakes from the rings, using a small spatula and transfer to serving plates. Decorate with slivered toasted almonds and slices of fresh lime, and serve.

VARIATION

If you prefer, substitute chopped dried apricots for the golden raisins.

Red Fruits with Foaming Sauce

A colorful combination of soft fruits, served with a frothy marshmallow sauce, is an ideal dessert when summer fruits are in season.

Serves 4

CALORIES PER SERVING: 220 • FAT CONTENT PER SERVING: 0.3 G

INGREDIENTS

8 ounces redcurrants, washed and trimmed, thawed if frozen

8 ounces cranberries

3 ounces light muscovado sugar

$^{3}/_{4}$ cup unsweetened apple juice

1 cinnamon stick, broken

$10^{1}/_{2}$ ounces small strawberries, washed, hulled and halved

SAUCE:

8 ounces raspberries, thawed if frozen

2 tbsp fruit cordial

$3^{1}/_{2}$ ounces marshmallows

1 Place the redcurrants, cranberries, and sugar in a saucepan. Pour in the apple juice and add the cinnamon stick. Bring the mixture to a boil and simmer gently for 10 minutes, until the fruit has just softened.

2 Stir the strawberries into the cranberry and sugar mixture and mix well. Transfer the mixture to a bowl, cover, and leave to chill in the refrigerator for about 1 hour. Remove and discard the cinnamon stick.

3 Just before serving, make the sauce. Place the raspberries and fruit cordial in a small saucepan, bring to a boil, and simmer for 2–3 minutes, until the fruit is just beginning to soften. Stir the marshmallows into the raspberry mixture and heat through, stirring, until the marshmallows begin to melt.

4 Transfer the fruit salad to serving bowls. Top with the raspberry and marshmallow sauce and serve.

VARIATION

This sauce is delicious poured over low-fat ice cream. For an extra-colorful sauce, replace the raspberries with an assortment of summer berries.

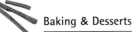

Brown Bread Ice Cream

Although it sounds unusual, this yogurt-based recipe is delicious.
It contains no cream and is ideal for a low-fat diet.

Serves 4

CALORIES PER SERVING: 265 • FAT CONTENT PER SERVING: 6 G

INGREDIENTS

6 ounces fresh whole-
  wheat breadcrumbs
1 ounce finely chopped walnuts
2 ounces superfine sugar
$\frac{1}{2}$ tsp ground nutmeg

1 tsp finely grated orange rind
2 cups low-fat unsweetened yogurt
2 large egg whites

TO DECORATE:
walnut halves
orange slices
fresh mint

1 Preheat the broiler. Mix the breadcrumbs, walnuts, and sugar together and spread over a sheet of foil in the broiler pan. Broil, stirring frequently, for 5 minutes until crisp and evenly browned. (Take care that the sugar does not burn.) Remove from the heat and allow to cool.

2 When the mixture is cool, transfer to a mixing bowl and mix in the nutmeg, orange rind, and yogurt. In another bowl, whisk the egg whites until stiff.

Gently fold the egg whites into the breadcrumb mixture using a metal spoon.

3 Spoon the mixture into 4 mini-basins, smooth over the tops, and freeze for 1½–2 hours until firm.

4 To serve, hold the bases of the molds in hot water for a few seconds, then turn onto serving plates. Serve immediately, decorated with a walnut half, orange rind, and fresh mint.

COOK'S TIP

If you don't have mini-basins, use ramekins or cups or, if you prefer, use one large bowl. Alternatively, spoon the mixture into a large, freezing container to freeze and serve the ice cream in scoops.

Chocolate Cheese Pots

These super-light desserts are just the thing if you have a craving for chocolate.
They're delicious served on their own or with a selection of fruits.

Serves 4

CALORIES PER SERVING: 170 • FAT CONTENT PER SERVING: 3 G

INGREDIENTS

1¼ cups low-fat ricotta cheese
²⁄₃ cup low-fat unsweetened yogurt
1 ounce confectioner's sugar
4 tsp low-fat drinking
   chocolate powder
4 tsp cocoa powder

1 tsp vanilla extract
2 tbsp dark rum (optional)
2 medium egg whites
4 chocolate cake decorations

TO SERVE:
pieces of kiwi fruit, orange,
   and banana
strawberries and raspberries

1   Combine the ricotta cheese and low-fat yogurt in a mixing bowl. Sift in the sugar, chocolate powder, and cocoa powder and mix until well combined. Add the vanilla extract and rum, if using.

2   In another bowl, whisk the egg whites until stiff. Using a metal spoon, fold the egg whites into the ricotta cheese, unsweetened yogurt, and chocolate mixture.

3   Spoon the ricotta cheese, unsweetened yogurt, and chocolate mixture into 4 small china dessert pots and chill in the refrigerator for about 30 minutes. Decorate each chocolate cheese pot with a chocolate cake decoration.

4   Serve each chocolate cheese pot with an assortment of fresh fruit, such as pieces of kiwi fruit, orange, and banana, and a few whole strawberries and raspberries.

VARIATION

This chocolate mixture would make an excellent filling for a cheesecake. Make the base out of crushed Amaretti di Saronno cookies and egg white, and set the filling with 2 tsp powdered gelatin dissolved in 2 tbsp boiling water. Make sure you use cookies made from apricot kernels, which are virtually fat free.

Citrus Meringue Crush

This is an excellent way to use up leftover meringue shells. It is very simple to prepare, yet tastes very luxurious. Serve with a spoonful of tangy fruit sauce.

Serves 4

CALORIES PER SERVING: 195 • FAT CONTENT PER SERVING: 0.6 G

INGREDIENTS

8 ready-made meringue nests
1¼ cups low-fat natural
   unsweetened yogurt
½ tsp finely grated orange rind
½ tsp finely grated lemon rind
½ tsp finely grated lime rind
2 tbsp orange liqueur or
   unsweetened orange juice

TO DECORATE:
sliced kumquat
lime rind, grated

SAUCE:
2 ounces kumquats
8 tbsp unsweetened orange juice
2 tbsp lemon juice

2 tbsp lime juice
2 tbsp water
2–3 tsp superfine sugar
1 tsp cornstarch mixed with
   1 tbsp water

1 Place the meringues in a clean plastic bag, seal the bag, and using a rolling pin, crush the meringues into small pieces. Transfer the crushed meringues to a mixing bowl.

2 Stir the yogurt, grated citrus rinds, and the liqueur or juice into the crushed meringue. Spoon the mixture into 4 mini-basins, smooth over the tops, and freeze for 1½–2 hours, until firm.

3 Meanwhile, make the sauce. Thinly slice the kumquats and place them in a small saucepan with the fruit juices and water. Bring gently to a boil and then simmer over a low heat for 3–4 minutes, until the kumquats have just softened.

4 Sweeten with sugar to taste, stir in the cornstarch mixture, and cook, stirring, until thickened. Pour into a small bowl, cover the surface with a layer of plastic wrap, and allow to cool—the film will help prevent a skin forming. Chill in the refrigerator until required.

5 To serve, dip the meringue basins in hot water for 5 seconds, or until they loosen, and turn onto serving plates. Spoon on a little sauce, decorate with slices of kumquat and lime rind, and serve immediately.

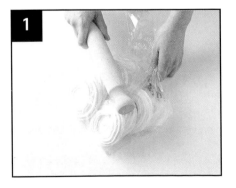

Tropical Fruit Fool

*Fruit fools are always popular, and this lightly tangy version will be
no exception. Use your favorite fruits in this recipe if you prefer.*

Serves 4

CALORIES PER SERVING: 170 • FAT CONTENT PER SERVING: 0.6 G

INGREDIENTS

1 medium ripe mango	$^1/_2$ tsp finely grated lime rind, plus extra to decorate	$^1/_2$ tsp vanilla extract
2 kiwi fruit		2 passion fruit
1 medium banana	2 medium egg whites	
2 tbsp lime juice	15 ounce can low-fat custard	

1 To peel the mango, slice either side of the smooth, flat central pit. Roughly chop the flesh and blend the fruit in a food processor or blender until smooth. Alternatively, mash with a fork.

2 Peel the kiwi fruit, chop the flesh into small pieces, and place in a bowl. Peel and chop the banana and add to the bowl. Toss all of the fruit in the lime juice and rind and mix well.

3 In a grease-free bowl, whisk the egg whites until stiff and then gently fold in the custard and vanilla extract until thoroughly mixed.

4 In 4 tall glasses, alternately layer the chopped fruit, mango purée, and custard mixture, finishing with the custard on top. Chill in the refrigerator for 20 minutes.

5 Halve the passion fruits, scoop out the seeds, and spoon the passion fruit over the fruit fools. Decorate each serving with the extra lime rind and serve.

VARIATION

Other tropical fruits to try include papaya purée, with chopped pineapple and dates, and tamarillo or pomegranate seeds to decorate. Or make a summer fruit fool by using strawberry purée, topped with raspberries and blackberries, with cherries to finish.

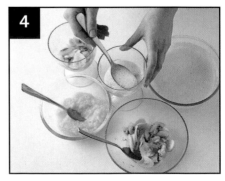

Brown Sugar Pavlovas

*This simple combination of fudgey meringue topped with
yogurt and raspberries is the perfect finale to any meal.*

Serves 4

CALORIES PER SERVING: 170 • FAT CONTENT PER SERVING: 0.2 G

INGREDIENTS

2 large egg whites
1 tsp cornstarch
1 tsp raspberry vinegar
3^1/$_2$ ounces light muscovado sugar,
 crushed free of lumps

^{3}/$_4$ cup low-fat unsweetened yogurt
6 ounces raspberries, thawed
 if frozen
2 tbsp redcurrant jelly

2 tbsp unsweetened orange juice
rose-scented geranium leaves,
 to decorate

1 Preheat the oven to 300°F.
Line a large cookie sheet with
baking parchment. In a large,
grease-free bowl, whisk the egg
whites until very stiff and dry. Fold
in the cornstarch and vinegar.

2 Gradually whisk in the sugar,
a spoonful at a time, until the
mixture is thick and glossy.

3 Divide the mixture into 4 and
spoon onto the cookie sheet,
spaced well apart. Smooth each
into a round, about 4 inches

across, and bake in the oven for
40–45 minutes until lightly
browned and crisp. Cool on the
cookie sheet.

4 Place the redcurrant jelly and
orange juice in a small
saucepan and heat, stirring, until
the jelly has melted. Cool for
10 minutes.

5 Meanwhile, using a spatula,
carefully remove each pavlova
from the baking parchment and
transfer to a serving plate. Top

with unsweetened yogurt and
raspberries.

6 Spoon on the redcurrant jelly
mixture to glaze. Decorate
and serve.

VARIATION

*Make a large pavlova
by forming the meringue into a
round, measuring 7 inches across,
on a lined cookie sheet
and bake for 1 hour.*

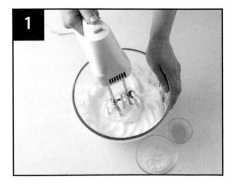

Apricot & Orange Jellies

These bright fruity little desserts are easy to make and taste so much better than store-bought jellies. Serve them with low-fat ice cream or a homemade whip.

Serves 4

CALORIES PER SERVING: 220 • FAT CONTENT PER SERVING: 4.5 G

INGREDIENTS

8 ounces no-need-to-soak
   dried apricots
1¼ cups unsweetened orange juice
2 tbsp lemon juice
2–3 tsp clear honey
1 tbsp powdered gelatin

4 tbsp boiling water

TO DECORATE:
orange segments
sprigs of mint

CINNAMON CREAM:
4 ounces medium fat ricotta cheese
4 ounces low-fat
   unsweetened yogurt
1 tsp ground cinnamon
1 tbsp clear honey

1 Place the apricots in a saucepan and pour in the orange juice. Bring to a boil, cover, and simmer for 15–20 minutes, until plump and soft. Set aside and cool for 10 minutes.

2 Transfer the mixture to a blender or food processor and blend until smooth. Stir in the lemon juice and add the honey. Measure the mixture and make 2½ cups with cold water.

3 Dissolve the gelatin in a boiling water and stir into the apricot mixture.

4 Pour the mixture into 4 individual molds, each ⅔ cup, or 1 large mold, 2½ cups. Chill until set.

5 Meanwhile, make the cinnamon cream. Thoroughly mix all the ingredients together and place in a small bowl. Cover and chill.

6 To turn out the jellies, dip the molds in hot water for a few seconds to loosen, and invert onto serving plates. Decorate and serve with the cinnamon cream dusted with extra cinnamon.

VARIATION

Other fruits that would work well in this recipe instead of the apricots are dried peaches, mangoes, and pears.

Sticky Sesame Bananas

These tasty morsels are a real treat. Pieces of banana are dipped in caramel and then sprinkled with a few sesame seeds.

Serves 4

CALORIES PER SERVING: 300 • FAT CONTENT PER SERVING: 4.5 G

INGREDIENTS

4 ripe medium bananas
3 tbsp lemon juice
4 ounces superfine sugar
4 tbsp cold water

2 tbsp sesame seeds
$^2/_3$ cup low-fat unsweetened yogurt
1 tbsp confectioner's sugar

1 tsp vanilla extract
lemon and lime rind, shredded,
   to decorate

1 Peel the bananas and cut into 2-inch pieces. Place the banana pieces in a bowl, add the lemon juice, and stir well to coat—this will help prevent the bananas from discoloring.

2 Place the sugar and water in a small saucepan and heat gently, stirring, until the sugar dissolves. Bring to a boil and cook for 5–6 minutes, until the mixture turns golden-brown.

3 Meanwhile, drain the bananas and blot with absorbent paper towels to dry. Line a cookie sheet or board with baking parchment and arrange the bananas, well spaced out, on top.

4 When the caramel is ready, drizzle it over the bananas, working quickly because the caramel sets almost instantly. Sprinkle with the sesame seeds and cool for 10 minutes.

5 Meanwhile, mix the unsweetened yogurt with the confectioner's sugar and vanilla extract.

6 Peel the bananas away from the paper and arrange on serving plates. Serve the unsweetened yogurt as a dip, decorated with the shredded lemon and lime rind.

COOK'S TIP

For best results, use a cannelle knife or a potato peeler to peel away thin strips of rind from the fruit, taking care not to include any bitter pith. Blanch the shreds in boiling water for 1 minute, then refresh in cold water.

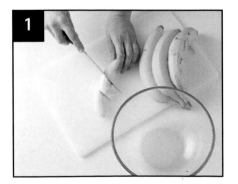

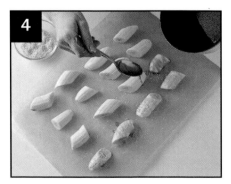

Mocha Swirl Mousse

*A combination of featherlight, yet rich, chocolate and coffee mousses, whipped
and set in serving glasses. These are definitely for a special occasion.*

Serves 4

CALORIES PER SERVING: 130 • FAT CONTENT PER SERVING: 6.5 G

INGREDIENTS

1 tbsp coffee and chicory essence
2 tsp cocoa powder, plus extra
   for dusting
1 tsp low-fat drinking
   chocolate powder

$^2/_3$ cup half-fat crème fraîche, plus
   4 tsp to serve (see Cook's Tip)
2 tsp powdered gelatin
2 tbsp boiling water
2 large egg whites

2 tbsp superfine sugar
4 chocolate coffee beans, to serve

1 Place the coffee and chicory essence in one bowl, and 2 tsp cocoa powder and the chocolate powder in another bowl. Divide the crème fraîche between the 2 bowls and mix both until well combined.

2 Dissolve the gelatin in the boiling water and set aside. In a grease-free bowl, whisk the egg whites and sugar until stiff, and divide this mixture evenly between the coffee mixture and the chocolate mixture.

3 Divide the dissolved gelatin between the 2 mixtures and, using a large metal spoon, gently fold until well mixed.

4 Spoon small amounts of the 2 mousses alternately into 4 serving glasses and swirl together gently. Chill for 1 hour or until set.

5 To serve, top each mousse with a teaspoonful of crème fraîche, a chocolate coffee bean, and a light dusting of cocoa powder. Serve immediately.

COOK'S TIP

Traditional crème fraîche is sour cream and has a fat content of around 40 percent. It is thick and has a slightly sour and nutty flavor. Lower-fat versions have a reduced fat content and are slightly looser in texture, but they should be used in a low-fat diet only occasionally. If you want to use a lower-fat alternative, a reduced fat, unsweetened yogurt would be more suitable.

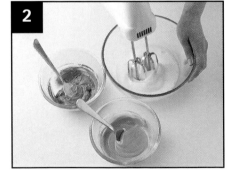

Fruit & Fiber Layers

A good, hearty dessert, guaranteed to fill you up.
Use your own favorite dried fruits in the compote.

Serves 4

CALORIES PER SERVING: 340 • FAT CONTENT PER SERVING: 6 G

INGREDIENTS

4 ounces dried apricots
4 ounces dried prunes
4 ounces dried peaches
2 ounces dried apple
1 ounce dried cherries
2 cups unsweetened apple juice

6 cardamom pods
6 cloves
1 cinnamon stick, broken
$3\frac{1}{4}$ cups low-fat
    unsweetened yogurt
14 ounces crunchy oat cereal

TO DECORATE:
apricot slices

1 To make the fruit compote, place the dried apricots, prunes, peaches, apples, and cherries in a saucepan and pour in the apple juice.

2 Add the cardamom pods, cloves, and cinnamon stick to the pan, bring to a boil, and simmer for 10–15 minutes, until the fruits are plump and tender.

3 Allow the mixture to cool completely in the pan, then transfer the mixture to a bowl, and leave to chill in the refrigerator for 1 hour. Remove and discard the spices from the fruits.

4 Spoon the compote into 4 dessert glasses, layering it alternately with yogurt and oat cereal, finishing with the oat cereal on top.

5 Decorate each dessert with slices of apricot and serve at once.

COOK'S TIP

There are many dried fruits available, including mangoes and pears, some of which need soaking, so read the instructions on the packet before use. Also, check the ingredients label, because several types of dried fruit have added sugar or are rolled in sugar, and this will affect the sweetness of the dish that you use them in.

Pan-cooked Apples in Red Wine

This simple combination of apples and raspberries cooked in red wine is a colorful and tempting dessert.

Serves 4

CALORIES PER SERVING: 200 • FAT CONTENT PER SERVING: 4.5 G

INGREDIENTS

4 eating apples
2 tbsp lemon juice
1¹/₂ ounces low-fat spread
2 ounces light muscovado sugar

1 small orange
1 cinnamon stick, broken
²/₃ cup red wine

8 ounces raspberries, hulled and
   thawed if frozen
sprigs of fresh mint, to decorate

1 Peel and core the apples, then cut them into thick wedges. Place the apples in a bowl and toss in the lemon juice to prevent the fruit from discoloring.

2 In a skillet, gently melt the low-fat spread over a low heat, add the sugar and stir to form a paste.

3 Stir the apple wedges into the pan and cook, stirring, for 2 minutes, until well coated in the sugar paste.

4 Using a vegetable peeler, pare off a few strips of orange rind. Add the orange rind to the pan, along with the cinnamon pieces. Extract the juice from the orange and pour into the pan with the red wine. Bring to a boil, then simmer for 10 minutes, stirring.

5 Add the raspberries to the pan and cook for 5 minutes, until the apples are tender.

6 Discard the orange rind and cinnamon pieces. Transfer the apple and raspberry mixture to a serving plate, together with the wine sauce. Decorate with a sprig of fresh mint and serve hot.

VARIATION

For other fruity combinations, cook the apples with blackberries, blackcurrants, or redcurrants. You may need to add more sugar if you use currants, as they are not as sweet as raspberries.

Mixed Fruit Brûlées

Traditionally a rich mixture made with cream, this fruit-based version is just as tempting. If you prefer, use unsweetened yogurt as a topping.

Serves 4

CALORIES PER SERVING: 225 • FAT CONTENT PER SERVING: 11 G

INGREDIENTS

1 pound prepared, assorted summer
   fruits (such as strawberries,
   raspberries, blackcurrants,
   redcurrants, and cherries), thawed
   if frozen

3/4 cup half-fat heavy
   cream alternative
3/4 cup low-fat unsweetened yogurt
1 tsp vanilla extract
4 tbsp raw crystal sugar

1 Divide the strawberries, raspberries, blackcurrants, redcurrants, and cherries evenly among 4 small, heatproof ramekin dishes.

2 Mix together the half-fat cream alternative, unsweetened yogurt, and vanilla extract. Generously spoon the mixture over the fruit.

3 Preheat the broiler. Top each serving with 1 tablespoon of brown crystal sugar and broil the desserts for 2–3 minutes, until the sugar melts and just begins to caramelize. Serve the brûlées piping hot.

VARIATION

If you are making this dessert for a special occasion, soak the fruits in 2–3 tbsp fruit liqueur before topping with the cream mixture.

COOK'S TIP

Look for half-fat creams, in light and heavy varieties. They are good substitutes for occasional use. Alternatively, in this recipe, omit the cream and double the quantity of yogurt for a lower-fat version.

Broiled Fruit Platter with Lime "Butter"

This delicious variation of a hot fruit salad includes wedges of tropical fruits, dusted with dark brown sugar and a pinch of spice before broiling.

Serves 4

CALORIES PER SERVING: 220 • FAT CONTENT PER SERVING: 6.5 G

INGREDIENTS

1 baby pineapple
1 ripe papaya
1 ripe mango
2 kiwi fruit
4 finger bananas

4 tbsp dark rum
1 tsp ground allspice
2 tbsp lime juice
4 tbsp dark muscovado sugar

LIME BUTTER:
2 ounces low-fat spread
$1/2$ tsp finely grated lime rind
1 tbsp confectioner's sugar

1 Quarter the pineapple, trimming away most of the leaves, and place in a shallow dish. Peel the papaya, cut it in half, and scoop out the seeds. Cut the flesh into thick wedges and place in the same dish as the pineapple.

2 Peel the mango, cut either side of the smooth, central flat pit and remove the pit. Slice the flesh into thick wedges. Peel the kiwi fruit and cut in half. Peel the bananas. Add all of these fruits to the dish.

3 Sprinkle with the rum, allspice, and lime juice, cover, and leave at room temperature for 30 minutes, turning occasionally, to allow the flavors to develop.

4 Meanwhile, make the butter. Place the low-fat spread in a small bowl and beat in the lime rind and sugar until well mixed. Chill until the butter is required.

5 Preheat the broiler. Drain the fruit, reserving the juices, and arrange in the broiler pan. Sprinkle with the sugar and broil for 3–4 minutes until hot and just beginning to char.

6 Transfer the fruit to a serving plate and spoon the juices on top. Serve with the lime butter.

VARIATION

Serve with a light sauce of 1 1/4 cups tropical fruit juice thickened with 2 tsp arrowroot.

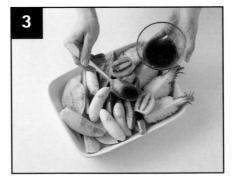

Baked Pears with Cinnamon & Brown Sugar

This simple recipe is easy to prepare and cook, but is deliciously warming. Serve hot with low-fat custard, or allow to cool and serve chilled with yogurt.

Serves 4

CALORIES PER SERVING: 160 • FAT CONTENT PER SERVING: 6 G

INGREDIENTS

4 ripe pears

2 tbsp lemon juice

4 tbsp light muscovado sugar

1 tsp ground cinnamon

2 ounces low-fat spread

low-fat custard, to serve

lemon rind, finely grated, to decorate

1 Preheat the oven to 400°F. Core and peel the pears, then slice them in half lengthwise, and brush all over with the lemon juice to prevent the pears from discoloring. Place the pears, cored side down, in a small nonstick roasting pan.

2 Place the sugar, cinnamon, and low-fat spread in a small saucepan and heat gently, stirring, until the sugar has melted. Keep the heat low to stop too much water evaporating from the low-fat spread as it gets hot. Spoon the mixture over the pears.

3 Bake for 20–25 minutes, or until the pears are tender and golden, occasionally spooning the sugar mixture over the fruit during the cooking time.

4 To serve, heat the custard until it is piping hot and spoon over the bases of 4 warm dessert plates. Arrange 2 pear halves on each plate. Decorate with grated lemon rind and serve.

VARIATION

This recipe also works well if you use cooking apples. For alternative flavors, replace the cinnamon with ground ginger, and serve the pears sprinkled with chopped, preserved ginger in syrup. Alternatively, use ground allspice and spoon warm dark rum on top.

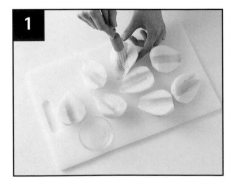

Baked Apples with Blackberries

This winter dessert is a classic dish. Large, fluffy apples are hollowed out and filled with spices, almonds, and blackberries. Serve hot with low-fat custard.

Serves 4

CALORIES PER SERVING: 250 • FAT CONTENT PER SERVING: 2 G

INGREDIENTS

4 medium-size cooking apples

1 tbsp lemon juice

3½ ounces prepared blackberries, thawed if frozen

½ ounce slivered almonds

½ tsp ground allspice

½ tsp finely grated lemon rind

2 tbsp raw crystal sugar

1¼ cups ruby port

1 cinnamon stick, broken

2 tsp cornstarch blended with 2 tbsp cold water

low-fat custard, to serve

1 Preheat the oven to 400°F. Wash and dry the apples. Using a small sharp knife, make a shallow cut through the skin around the middle of each apple—this will help the apples to cook through.

2 Core the apples, brush the centers with the lemon juice to prevent browning, and stand in a shallow ovenproof dish.

3 In a bowl, mix together the blackberries, almonds, allspice, lemon rind, and sugar. Using a teaspoon, spoon the mixture into the center of each apple.

4 Pour the port into the dish, add the cinnamon stick, and bake the apples in the oven for 35–40 minutes, or until tender and soft. Drain the cooking juices into a pan and keep the apples warm.

5 Discard the cinnamon and add the cornstarch mixture to the cooking juices. Heat, stirring, until thickened.

6 Heat the custard until piping hot. Pour the sauce over the apples and serve with the custard.

VARIATION

Use raspberries instead of blackberries and, if you prefer, replace the port with unsweetened orange juice.

White Lace Crêpes with Oriental Fruits

*These super-light crêpes melt in the mouth. They are filled
with a gingered fruit salad of melon, grapes, and lychees.*

Serves 4

CALORIES PER SERVING: 170 • FAT CONTENT PER SERVING: 1.5 G

INGREDIENTS

3 medium egg whites
4 tbsp cornstarch
3 tbsp cold water
1 tsp vegetable oil

FILLING:
12 ounces fresh lychees
$1/4$ Galia melon
6 ounces seedless green grapes

$1/2$-inch piece fresh root ginger
2 pieces preserved ginger in syrup
2 tbsp ginger wine *or* dry sherry

1 To make the fruit filling, peel the lychees and remove the pits. Place the lychees in a bowl. Scoop out the seeds from the melon and remove the skin. Cut the melon flesh into small pieces and place in the bowl.

2 Wash and dry the grapes, remove from the stalks, and add to the bowl. Peel the ginger root and cut into thin shreds or grate finely. Drain the preserved ginger pieces, reserving the syrup, and chop the ginger pieces finely.

3 Mix the gingers into the bowl, along with the ginger wine or sherry and the reserved preserved ginger syrup. Cover and set aside.

4 Meanwhile, prepare the crêpes. In a small pitcher, mix together the egg whites, cornstarch, and cold water until very smooth.

5 Brush a small nonstick crêpe pan with oil and heat until hot. Drizzle the surface of the pan with a quarter of the cornstarch mixture to give a lacy effect. Cook for a few seconds until set, then carefully lift out, and transfer to absorbent paper towels to drain. Set aside and keep warm. Repeat with the remaining mixture to make 4 crêpes in total.

6 To serve, place a crêpe on each serving plate and top with the fruit filling. Fold over the pancake and serve hot.

Fruit Loaf with Strawberry & Apple Spread

This sweet, fruity loaf is ideal served with coffee or as a healthy snack.

Serves 8

CALORIES PER SERVING: 360 • FAT CONTENT PER SERVING: 2.8 G

INGREDIENTS

6 ounces oatmeal
3¹/₂ ounces light muscovado sugar
1 tsp ground cinnamon
4¹/₂ ounces golden raisins
6 ounces seedless raisins
2 tbsp malt extract
1¹/₄ cups unsweetened apple juice

6 ounces self-rising whole-
  wheat flour
1¹/₂ tsp baking powder
strawberries and apple wedges,
  to serve

FRUIT SPREAD:
8 ounces strawberries, washed
  and hulled
2 eating apples, cored, chopped, and
  mixed with 1 tbsp lemon juice to
  prevent browning
1¹/₄ cups unsweetened apple juice

1 Preheat the oven to 350°F. Grease and line a 2-pound loaf pan. Place the oatmeal, sugar, cinnamon, golden raisins, raisins, and malt extract in a mixing bowl. Pour in the apple juice, stir well, and let soak for 30 minutes.

2 Sift in the flour and baking powder, adding any husks that remain in the strainer, and fold in using a metal spoon. Spoon the mixture into the prepared pan and bake for 1½ hours, until firm or until a skewer inserted into the center comes out clean. Cool for 10 minutes, then turn onto a rack, and cool completely.

3 Meanwhile, make the fruit spread. Place the strawberries and apples in a saucepan and pour in the apple juice. Bring to a boil, cover, and simmer for 30 minutes. Beat the sauce well and spoon into a clean, warmed jar. Set aside and let cool, then seal and label the jar.

4 Serve the loaf with 1–2 tablespoons of the fruit spread and an assortment of strawberries and apple wedges.

Banana & Lime Cake

A substantial loaf-type cake that is ideal served with coffee. The mashed bananas help to keep the cake moist, and it is drizzled with a lime frosting for extra zing and zest.

Serves 10

CALORIES PER SERVING: 360 • FAT CONTENT PER SERVING: 2.8 G

INGREDIENTS

10¹/₂ ounces all-purpose flour
1 tsp salt
1¹/₂ tsp baking powder
6 ounces light muscovado sugar
1 tsp lime rind, grated
1 medium egg, beaten

1 medium banana, mashed with
  1 tbsp lime juice
²/₃ cup low-fat unsweetened yogurt
4 ounces golden raisins
banana chips, to decorate
lime rind, finely grated, to decorate

TOPPING:
4 ounces confectioner's sugar
1–2 tsp lime juice
¹/₂ tsp lime rind, finely grated

1 Preheat the oven to 350°F. Grease and line a deep 7-inch round cake pan with baking parchment. Sift the flour, salt, and baking powder into a mixing bowl and stir in the sugar and lime rind until well combined.

2 Make a well in the center of the dry ingredients and add the egg, banana, yogurt, and golden raisins. Mix well until thoroughly incorporated.

3 Spoon the mixture into the pan and smooth the surface. Bake for 40–45 minutes, until firm to the touch or until a skewer inserted in the center comes out clean. Cool for 10 minutes, then turn out onto a wire rack.

4 To make the topping, sift the confectioner's sugar into a small bowl and mix with the lime juice to form a soft, but not too runny, frosting. Stir in the lime

rind. Drizzle the frosting over the cake, letting it run down the sides.

5 Decorate with banana chips and lime rind. Let stand for 15 minutes, so that the frosting sets.

VARIATION

Replace the lime rind and juice with orange, and the golden raisins with chopped apricots.

Crispy Sugar-topped Blackberry & Apple Cake

The sugar cubes give a lovely crunchy top to this moist bake.

Serves 10

CALORIES PER SERVING: 230 • FAT CONTENT PER SERVING: 1.5 G

INGREDIENTS

12 ounces cooking apples
3 tbsp lemon juice
10 1/2 ounces self-rising whole-
    wheat flour
1/2 tsp baking powder
1 tsp ground cinnamon, plus extra
    for dusting

6 ounces prepared blackberries,
    thawed if frozen, plus extra to
    decorate
6 ounces light muscovado sugar
1 medium egg, beaten

3/4 cup low-fat unsweetened yogurt
2 ounces white or brown sugar
    cubes, lightly crushed
sliced eating apple,
    to decorate

1 Preheat the oven to 375°F. Grease and line a 2-pound loaf pan. Core, peel, and finely dice the apples. Place them in a saucepan with the lemon juice, bring to a boil, cover, and simmer for 10 minutes, until soft and pulpy. Beat well and set aside to cool.

2 Sift the flour, baking powder, and 1 tsp cinnamon into a bowl, adding any husks that remain in the strainer. Stir in 4 ounces blackberries and the sugar.

3 Make a well in the center of the ingredients and add the egg, unsweetened yogurt, and cooled apple purée. Mix well to incorporate thoroughly. Spoon the mixture into the prepared loaf pan and smooth over the top.

4 Sprinkle with the remaining blackberries, pressing them down into the cake mixture, and top with the crushed sugar lumps. Bake for 40–45 minutes. Cool in the pan.

5 Remove the cake from the pan and peel away the lining paper. Serve dusted with cinnamon and decorated with extra blackberries and apple slices.

Rich Fruit Cake

This moist cake would also make an excellent Christmas cake.

Serves 12

CALORIES PER SERVING: 315 • FAT CONTENT PER SERVING: 3 G

INGREDIENTS

6 ounces unsweetened pitted dates
4 ounces dried prunes
$^3/_4$ cup unsweetened orange juice
2 tbsp molasses
1 tsp finely grated lemon rind
1 tsp finely grated orange rind
8 ounces self-rising
   whole wheat flour

1 tsp apple pie spice
4 ounces seedless raisins
4 ounces golden sultanas
4 ounces currants
4 ounces dried cranberries
3 large eggs, separated
confectioner's sugar

TO DECORATE:
1 tbsp apricot preserves, softened,
6 ounces sugar paste
strips of orange rind
strips of lemon rind

1 Preheat the oven to 325°F. Grease and line a deep 8-inch round cake pan. Chop the dates and prunes and place in a pan. Add the orange juice and bring to a boil. Simmer for 10 minutes until very soft.

2 Remove the pan from the heat and beat the fruit mixture until puréed. Stir in the molasses and citrus rinds until well combined. Set aside and let cool.

3 Meanwhile, sift the flour and apple pie spice into a bowl, adding any husks that remain in the strainer. Mix in the dried fruits and make a well in the center.

4 When the date and prune mixture is cool, whisk in the egg yolks. In a separate bowl, whisk the egg whites until stiff. Spoon the fruit and egg yolk mixture into the dry ingredients, and gradually work together using a wooden spoon.

5 Gently fold in the egg whites, using a metal spoon. Transfer to the prepared pan and bake for 1½ hours. Cool completely in the pan.

6 Remove the cake from the pan and brush the top with preserves. Dust the counter with confectioner's sugar and roll out the sugar paste thinly. Lay the sugar paste over the top of the cake and trim the edges. Decorate the cake with orange and lemon rind.

Carrot & Ginger Cake

This melt-in-the-mouth version has a fraction of the fat of the traditional cake.

Serves 10

CALORIES PER SERVING: 300 • FAT CONTENT PER SERVING: 10 G

INGREDIENTS

8 ounces all-purpose flour
1 tsp baking powder
1 tsp baking soda
2 tsp ground ginger
$^1/_2$ tsp salt
6 ounces light muscovado sugar
8 ounces carrots, grated
2 pieces preserved ginger in syrup,
   drained and chopped
1 ounce fresh ginger root, grated

2 ounces seedless raisins
2 medium eggs, beaten
3 tbsp corn oil
juice of 1 medium orange

TO DECORATE:
grated carrot
preserved ginger
ground ginger

FROSTING:
8 ounces low-fat soft cheese
4 tbsp confectioner's sugar
1 tsp vanilla extract

1 Preheat the oven to 350°F. Grease and line an 8-inch round cake pan with baking parchment.

2 Sift the flour, baking powder, baking soda, ground ginger, and salt into a mixing bowl. Stir in the sugar, carrot, preserved ginger, fresh root ginger, and raisins. Make a well in the center of the dry ingredients.

3 Beat together the eggs, oil, and orange juice, then pour into the center of the well. Combine the ingredients together until well mixed.

4 Spoon the mixture into the pan and smooth the surface. Bake in the oven for 1–1¼ hours, until firm to the touch, or until a skewer inserted into the center comes out clean. Cool in the pan.

5 To make the frosting, place the soft cheese in a bowl and beat to soften. Sift in the confectioner's sugar and add the vanilla extract. Stir until well combined.

6 Remove the cake from the pan and smooth the frosting over the top. Serve decorated with grated carrot, preserved ginger, and a dusting of ground ginger.

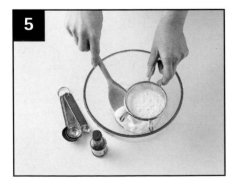

Strawberry Roulade

The light, moist sponge rolled up with an almond and strawberry yogurt filling is not strictly a roulade—it contains flour—but the result is similar.

Serves 8

CALORIES PER SERVING: 185 • FAT CONTENT PER SERVING: 4 G

INGREDIENTS

3 large eggs
4 ounces superfine sugar
4 ounces all-purpose flour
1 tbsp hot water

FILLING:
$^3/_4$ cup low-fat unsweetened yogurt
1 tsp almond extract
8 ounces small strawberries

$^1/_2$ ounce toasted
  almonds, slivered
1 tsp confectioner's sugar

1 Preheat the oven to 425°F. Line a 14 x 10-inch jelly roll pan with baking parchment. Place the eggs in a mixing bowl with the superfine sugar. Place the bowl over a pan of hot water and whisk until pale and thick.

2 Remove the bowl from the pan. Sift in the flour and fold into the eggs with the hot water. Pour the mixture into the pan and bake for 8–10 minutes, until golden and set.

3 Transfer the mixture to a sheet of baking parchment. Peel off the lining paper and roll up the sponge tightly along with the baking parchment. Wrap in a dish cloth and let cool.

4 To make the filling, mix together the yogurt and almond extract. Reserving a few strawberries for decoration, wash, hull, and slice the rest. Leave the filling mixture to chill until ready to assemble.

5 Unroll the sponge, spread the yogurt mixture over the sponge, and sprinkle with strawberries. Roll the sponge up again and transfer to a serving plate. Sprinkle with the almonds and lightly dust with confectioner's sugar. Decorate with the reserved strawberries.

VARIATION

Serve the roulade with a fruit purée, sweetened with a little sugar.

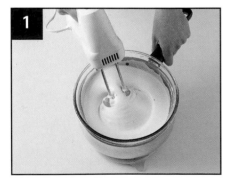

Fruity Muffins

Another American favorite, these little cakes contain no butter, just a little corn oil.

Makes 10

CALORIES PER SERVING: 180 • FAT CONTENT PER SERVING: 1.5 G

INGREDIENTS

8 ounces self-rising whole-
  wheat flour
2 tsp baking powder
1 ounce light muscovado sugar
3$^1/_2$ ounces dried apricots,
  finely chopped

1 medium banana, mashed with
  1 tbsp orange juice
1 tsp orange rind, grated finely
1$^1/_4$ cups skim milk
1 medium egg, beaten
3 tbsp corn oil

2 tbsp oatmeal
fruit spread, honey, or maple syrup,
  to serve

1 Preheat the oven to 400°F. Place 10 paper muffin cups in a deep muffin pan.

2 Sift the flour and baking powder into a mixing bowl, adding any husks that remain in the strainer. Stir in the sugar and chopped apricots and mix until well combined.

3 Make a well in the center of the dry ingredients and add the banana, orange rind, milk, beaten egg, and oil. Mix together well to form a thick batter. Divide the batter evenly among the 10 paper cups.

4 Sprinkle with a little oatmeal and bake for 25–30 minutes, until well risen and firm to the touch, or until a toothpick inserted into the center comes out clean. Transfer the muffins to a wire rack to cool slightly.

5 Serve the muffins warm with a little fruit spread, honey, or maple syrup.

VARIATION

If you like dried figs, they make a deliciously crunchy alternative to the apricots; they also go very well with the flavor of orange. Other no-need-to-soak dried fruits, chopped up finely, can be used as well. Store these muffins in an airtight container for 3-4 days. They also freeze well in sealed bags or in freezer containers for up to 3 months.

Chocolate Brownies

*Yes, you really can have a low-fat chocolate treat. These moist bars incorporate
a dried fruit purée, which enables you to bake without adding any fat.*

Makes 12

CALORIES PER SERVING: 300 • FAT CONTENT PER SERVING: 4.5 G

INGREDIENTS

2 ounces unsweetened pitted
  dates, chopped
2 ounces dried prunes, chopped
6 tbsp unsweetened apple juice
4 medium eggs, beaten
10^1/$_2$ ounces dark muscovado sugar
1 tsp vanilla extract

4 tbsp low-fat drinking chocolate
  powder, plus extra for dusting
2 tbsp cocoa powder
6 ounces all-purpose flour
2 ounces plain chocolate chips

FROSTING:
4 ounces confectioner's sugar
1–2 tsp water
1 tsp vanilla extract

1 Preheat the oven to 350°F.
Grease and line a 7 x 11-inch
cake pan with baking parchment.
Place the dates and prunes in a
small saucepan and add the apple
juice. Bring to a boil, cover, and
simmer for 10 minutes, until soft.
Beat to form a smooth paste, then
set aside to cool.

2 Place the cooled fruit in a
mixing bowl and stir in the
eggs, sugar, and vanilla extract. Sift

in 4 tbsp chocolate powder, the
cocoa, and the flour, and fold in,
along with the chocolate chips,
until well incorporated.

3 Spoon the mixture into the
prepared pan and smooth
over the top. Bake for
25–30 minutes until firm to the
touch or until a toothpick inserted
into the center of the cake comes
out clean. Cut into 12 bars and
cool in the pan for 10 minutes.

Transfer to a wire rack to cool
completely.

4 To make the frosting, sift the
sugar into a bowl and mix
with sufficient water and the
vanilla extract to form a soft, but
not too runny, frosting.

5 Drizzle the frosting over the
chocolate brownies and allow
to set. Dust with the extra
chocolate powder before serving.

Cheese & Chive Biscuits

These little classics have been given a healthy twist by the use of low-fat soft cheese and reduced-fat Cheddar cheese. They're just as delicious, however. Serve warm for the best flavor.

Makes 10

CALORIES PER SERVING: 120 • FAT CONTENT PER SERVING: 2.8 G

INGREDIENTS

9 ounces self-rising flour
1 tsp powdered mustard
½ tsp cayenne pepper
½ tsp salt

3½ ounces low-fat soft cheese with added herbs
2 tbsp fresh snipped chives, plus extra to garnish

3½ fl ounces and 2 tbsp skim milk
2 ounces reduced-fat cheddar cheese, grated
low-fat soft cheese, to serve

1 Preheat the oven to 400°F. Sift the flour, mustard, cayenne pepper, and salt into a mixing bowl.

2 Add the soft cheese to the mixture and mix together until well incorporated. Stir in the snipped chives.

3 Make a well in the center of the ingredients and gradually pour in 3½ fl ounces milk, stirring as you pour, until the mixture forms a soft dough.

4 Turn the dough onto a floured counter and knead lightly. Roll out until ¾ inch thick and use a 2-inch plain pastry cutter to stamp out as many rounds as you can. Transfer the rounds to a cookie sheet.

5 Re-knead the dough trimmings together and roll out again. Stamp out more rounds—you should be able to make 10 biscuits in total.

6 Brush the biscuits with the remaining milk and sprinkle with the grated cheese. Bake for 15–20 minutes, until risen and golden. Transfer to a wire rack to cool. Serve warm with low-fat soft cheese, garnished with chives.

VARIATION

For a sweet variation omit the mustard, cayenne, chives, and grated cheese and add 3 ounces currants or raisins and 1 ounce sugar, and use plain low-fat soft cheese.

Savory Tomato & Bell Pepper Bread

This flavorsome bread contains only the minimum amount of fat.

Serves 8

CALORIES PER SERVING: 250 • FAT CONTENT PER SERVING: 3 G

INGREDIENTS

1 small red bell pepper
1 small green bell pepper
1 small yellow bell pepper
2 ounces dry-pack sun-
   dried tomatoes
$^1/_4$ cup boiling water

2 tsp dried yeast
1 tsp superfine sugar
$^2/_3$ cup tepid water
1 pound strong white bread flour
2 tsp dried rosemary
2 tbsp tomato paste

$^2/_3$ cup low-fat unsweetened yogurt
1 tbsp coarse salt
1 tbsp olive oil

1 Preheat the oven to 425°F and the broiler to hot. Halve and seed the bell peppers, arrange on the broiler rack, and cook until the skin is charred. Leave to cool for 10 minutes, peel off the skin, and chop the flesh.

2 Slice the tomatoes into strips, place in a heatproof bowl, and add the boiling water. Set aside to soak.

3 Place the yeast and sugar in a small pitcher, add the water, and leave for about

10–15 minutes, until frothy. Sift the flour into a bowl and add 1 tsp dried rosemary. Make a well in the center and pour in the yeast mixture.

4 Add the tomato paste, the tomatoes and soaking liquid, the bell peppers, yogurt, and half the salt. Mix together to form a soft dough.

5 Turn the dough out onto a lightly floured counter and knead for 3–4 minutes, until smooth and elastic. Place in a

lightly floured bowl, cover, and leave in a warm room for about 40 minutes, until doubled in size.

6 Knead the dough again and place in a lightly greased, 9-inch round, spring-form cake pan. Using a wooden spoon, form "dimples" in the surface. Cover and leave for 30 minutes.

7 Brush with oil and sprinkle with rosemary and salt. Bake for 35–40 minutes, cool for 10 minutes, and release from the pan. Cool on a rack.

Index